COOKING
for a
HEALTHY
FAMILY

COOKING
for a
HEALTHY
FAMILY

SIMON HOPE

Photography by Sara Taylor

STEWART, TABORI & CHANG
NEW YORK

Published in 1995 and distributed in the U.S.
by Stewart, Tabori and Chang,
a division of U.S. Media Holdings, INC.
575 Broadway, New York, N.Y. 10012

Distributed in Canada by
General Publishing Co. Ltd.
30 Lesmill Road, Don Mills, Ontario
Canada, M3B 2T6

First published in Great Britain in 1995
by Mitchell Beazley, an imprint of Reed
Consumer Books Ltd.

ISBN 1-55670-427-5

Library of Congress Catalog Card Number:
95-69565.

Printed in Hong Kong

ACKNOWLEDGEMENTS
Art Director Jacqui Small
Designer Barbara Zuniga
Executive Editor Susan Haynes
Editor Kathy Steer
Production Controller Melanie Frantz
Photographer Sara Taylor

NOTES

Eggs should be from free-range chickens
and medium size unless otherwise stated.
Whole milk should be used unless
otherwise stated.
Shoyu is Japanese soy sauce
Nibbed is tiny dice.

Ovens should be preheated to the specified
temperature–if using a convection oven,
follow the manufacturer's instructions for
adjusting the time and temperature.

I'd like to say a big thank you to my family, especially Kate for bravely cooking where no one has cooked before. To Daisy for honesty, Hamish for his taste buds and Mollie for eating up everything on her plate!

CONTENTS

INTRODUCTION

Don't worry, you're normal. You have a healthy interest in good food, you may or may not be vegetarian but one thing is for sure; you care. Picking up this book and getting this far deserves a reward. Now read on, you're in good company.

I have been in the vegetarian restaurant business for 18 years now–almost all of my working life–and I still really love it and the food we create. But unlike when I started, I now have a family of my own. Three times Kate has grown large; successfully given birth and nursed our children–Daisy, Hamish and Mollie. Three times she has produced the most delightful, happy, healthy and vibrant offspring. "Not bad for a vegetarian," some people say, as if the only sure way of breeding healthy humans is on a diet of meat and fish.

It became obvious to me that a cookbook was needed for families, a book to banish the misconceptions inbred by a meat-obsessed society, a book to turn the tables and suggest that it is probably best not to eat meat when pregnant and nursing. It is far healthier and less dangerous to have a meat-free diet so long as your vegetarian diet is fully comprehensive. Human beings were definitely never designed to eat so much meat, let alone meat that comes from animals pumped with chemicals and growth hormones. A pregnant or nursing mother should eat food as pure as possible. *Cooking for a Healthy Family* probes to the very heart of family cooking, covering the practicalities of feeding a vegetarian family through the early years and onto school and out the other side.

I'm a great lover of France (although the French, in general, have absolutely no concept of vegetarian food) and a few years ago I dropped in at a convenient farmhouse to buy a few quarts of local wine. At the huge kitchen table worked an equally huge woman filling yards of intestine with ground pork to make huge sausages. In my broken French I managed a reasonably humorous and, I thought, eloquent conversation, the gist of which was about their pig, which they had killed three weeks earlier. The last bits of it were going into the sausages. Such sound and frugal housekeeping has more in common with life in the 17th century than today: they killed their pig because they needed the meat and you can bet your last nut cutlet that not one part of the animal was wasted or unappreciated.

The number of people in England who are wholly or partly vegetarian or vegan is growing at a meteoric rate and it's not just because they don't like the idea of eating animals. Often it has more to do with a dislike of how the animals have been reared, what they were given to eat, what drugs made them grow larger and leaner, what it tastes like and whether our bodies really need it. After all, it is not usually our pig.

I have a lot of friends who, on principle, would never touch vegetarian food—they "like their meat." A closer examination shows that these people actually don't like their meat. Unlike the French farming wife, who valued her pig (and every last bit of it, too) these so called "carnivores" balk at any part of the animal that doesn't come neatly wrapped in a supermarket package clearly designed to minimize the chance of them actually having to touch the real thing. It has always seemed strangely paradoxical to me that most carnivores will happily eat a cow's bottom but not its head. And when it comes to cooking, what do these meat eaters do to their meat? They render it tasteless by overcooking it.

If the truth be known, the English are a nation of vegetarians waiting to come out of the closet. We've lost touch with animal husbandry and we are frightened of being shown the level and types of slaughter that take place every day so that we can overcook this meat.

In the past, people fought for meat, but then it was a rare treat. Meat symbolized health, wealth, happiness and security in a time when life itself was more uncertain. For the common people it was often an unobtainable goal which, if achieved, was seen as a buffer against the harsh physical existence of a world in which there were no luxuries or labor-saving devices.

The 20th century has brought with it plenty of meat for us Westerners, as well as every luxury and labor-saving device. The symbolic desire for meat has remained intact but the actual need has completely disappeared. Consequently,

meat itself has become a killer–heart disease, bowel disease and obesity have become the biggest threat to us–far more so than AIDS. Is it any surprise that so many people are becoming vegetarian? If meat ever becomes popular again, it'll be because some future society will ensure that we all have our own pig or cow to tend, love and finally eat.

In writing this book I have talked to parents whose children suffer from a wide variety of illnesses, from simple allergies through asthma to autism. Without exception they all wish they had appreciated the importance of diet before having children. There's not a lot we can do about our genetic structure (yet), but we can get the best from our bodies by altering what we eat and, especially when pregnant and in the vital first 18 months after birth, during which time our vital organs develop along with our immune systems. Nowadays it is very easy for pregnant women and young mothers to opt for nutritious diets which are full of organic foods that are particularly designed for their own bodies.

I hope you enjoy *Cooking for a Healthy Family*. I've had great fun writing it and I hope that it will help you and your family have a happier and healthier life.

EQUIPMENT, COOKING TECHNIQUES AND INGREDIENTS

EQUIPMENT

Knives

Use the right knife for you and life as a vegetarian cook will be more fun. On the whole vegetarians have to prepare more vegetables and fruit than their meat-eating counterparts, who can just slam a rib on the barbecue, sit back and relax.

I use a Japanese vegetable chopping knife. It has a square nose, good balance and is very sharp. Our head chef, Karen, at Food For Friends, prefers a huge pointed knife.

Practice chopping vegetables like zucchini or cucumbers with the fingers of the non-knife wielding hand well tucked in, while at the same time keeping the vegetable or fruit firmly in place. Let the last knuckle of the middle finger act as a guide against which the knife goes up and down.

Vegetables and fruits will be cut according to their role in the dish, be it to lie flat, stand square or just look pretty. Always wash them well before use, except mushrooms, which should just be brushed to remove any dirt (water makes mushrooms soggy). Waxed fruits like oranges should be scrubbed first in hot water if the peel is to be used. Waxed cucumbers must have their skins removed, unless organically grown–the wax holds in chemical sprays. Remove all damaged or blighted parts of fruits and vegetables. Knives must be sharpened, preferably after each use to maintain a perfect edge. Equally, after use they should be stored very carefully on a magnetic strip or in a wooden block to avoid damaging their sharpness.

Pots and Pans

Keep pots and pans clean and dry. Most metal dishes start to suffer metal fatigue simply because they are not dried properly. If they don't have plastic handles the best way to dry them is in the oven. It is a very tempting but false economy to buy cheap cookware. Thick gauge stainless steel lined with copper will last a lifetime although it is not necessary in the case of pans for boiling or steaming. Burned pots should be scoured only with salt and lemon juice.

Cooking Vegetables and Fruit

The art of cooking vegetables is to preserve their flavor, texture and nutritional benefits. Generally, fruit should be prepared at the last moment as fruit is prone to lose water, shape and color very quickly after preparation.

There are several different cooking techniques involved as described below.

Boiling

Boiling is a technique used less and less. First bring lightly salted water to a boil, add the unfortunate vegetables and bring to a boil again before lowering the heat to a gentle rolling boil. Remove the vegetables before they are tender as they will continue to cook afterwards. Save the liquid to use as stock or for cooking more vegetables.

Steaming

Steaming is much more in vogue these days as the end result has greater flavor and higher nutrients. Buy a cheap bamboo Chinese system that will fit one of your pans. Different liquids will give the food being steamed subtly different flavors.

Stir-frying or sautéing

These are probably the most common methods used in vegetarian cooking. Heat the pan first, add the oil or butter and remove from the heat if it gets very hot to avoid burning. Toss and stir the vegetables into the oil or butter and make sure each is evenly coated. The combination of hot oil and hot pan will for a time seal in the flavor of the vegetables. If you are not able to toss the vegetables in the pan use a wooden spoon and stir them.

Roasting

This is definitely the most up and coming technique in vegetarian cooking. In the past only root vegetables and certain bulbs were commonly roasted. Now eggplant, bell peppers, zucchini, tomatoes, onions, shallots, garlic, fennel and even asparagus are quite commonly roasted. The basic rules apply. Vegetables have very little natural fat so more must be added; any oil will do but I like extra-virgin olive oil best. Try adding your favorite dried herbs and seasonings. Heat a little oil in a roasting pan, brush the vegetables to be roasted with oil and sprinkle on salt and pepper and anything else you fancy. Quickly sauté in a stove-top safe casserole before transferring to a hot oven. Some people peel roasted peppers and eggplants, but unless they are completely blackened I can't see the point. When roasting garlic it's best to use fresh garlic.

Ingredients

Herbs

Always use fresh herbs when available. Soft, leafy herbs like basil are best added at the end of the cooking process while "hard" leaves like bay are best added at the beginning. Smaller-leaved fresh herbs can be added whenever called for. Dried herbs should be revitalized by rubbing between the palms of your hands. This reactivates the enriched oils in them and helps bring more flavor to the dish. Always keep dried herbs in a cool dark place and fresh herbs like flowers in a vase of water.

Spices

If you use freshly ground spices, grind them in a coffee grinder dedicated to spices and clean out thoroughly after each use. Ground spices must be kept cool and in a dark place or jar. Ground spices are fat-soluble and so must always be added at the stir-fry stage of a dish. Pepper is a spice and you should use freshly ground black pepper.

Dried beans, peas and grains

Most beans and some peas should be well soaked before cooking. Cooking times will vary according to how long they have been soaked and how old they are.

Garlic

Once a week peel a whole bulb or two of garlic and keep covered with extra-virgin olive oil. Not only do you then have instant fresh garlic, at the end of the week you also have garlic-flavored olive oil—yummy!

Leeks, watercress and spinach

These are notoriously dirty vegetables so take great care to wash them thoroughly—be quick preparing spinach or use iced water as it wilts quickly.

Green potatoes

If you're pregnant or nursing do not eat green potatoes.

Cream

Sauces made with cream are a lovely treat. Remember that as vegetarians you probably eat 50% less fat than meat eaters anyway. If you can get it use organic cream.

Storage and Nutritional Considerations

Storage

Quite simply, fresh is best but a little careful handling can extend the life of fruit and vegetables. They are best stored in a cool, dark place. Light and heat destroy their delicate systems, which begin to decay the moment they are picked. Throw out any glass storage jars and replace them with cans or pottery jars. If possible, keep excess vegetables in the garage or basement; funnily enough, refrigerators can hasten the demise of fruit and vegetables as much as heat. Three to four days is the maximum length of time for which most vegetables or fruits can be refrigerated. Never refrigerate potatoes, bananas or citrus fruits, unless cut.

With the exception of frozen peas, corn, lima beans and some fruits, freezers are best used for finished products such as pre-prepared meals, sauces, purées and stocks.

Some fruits and vegetables are best preserved in oil or vinegar, or simply sun-dried. In these cases they usually take on a new identity and become more of an ingredient than they were originally.

Nutrition

Proteins: Vegetarians get protein from many sources but I believe the best source is a combination of beans, grains and cereals.

Fats: Don't use margarine, use butter or cold-pressed extra-virgin olive oils. Butter is a completely natural product and if eaten in small quantities can do no harm. Margarine is altogether different—I'm sure that the manufacturing techniques, even of pure vegetable margarine, is suspect. (Remember that fat children become fat adults.)

Vitamins and minerals: To ensure a good intake of vitamins and minerals, simply eat a good variety of fresh food that has been cooked at home. Do not become a food faddist. There is no need to take vitamin or mineral supplements unless you have been ill.

Carbohydrates: The powerhouse of our diet and one area where vegetarians can't fail. Nearly all the basics in a vegetarian diet contain large amounts of carbohydrates and that vital other ingredient, dietary fiber, needed for a healthy digestive and immune system.

JUST THE TWO OF US
OR LIFE BEFORE CHILDREN (BC) AND OCCASIONALLY AFTER

For many of us, life before children seems a somewhat distant memory, with strange habits such as "lying in bed in the morning," "staying awake until well past midnight," and even more outrageously "not having to cook," forming the bedrock of existence.

Dinner parties, of course, are as much a part and parcel of family life after children as they were BC, although generally by the time you and your partner have had a couple of children these nocturnal home entertainments have become rather slick affairs. It is here that you must be careful—all too often couples can become too well organized. There is nothing worse than going to dinner with the "Lasagne People" or the "Curry Couple," who, despite being kind and generous, never seem to realize that every time you go to eat there that magical element of surprise is always missing. More importantly, your guests might not particularly like lasagne or curry! Of course, there's always the clever host who records all details of a dinner party–who came to dinner and what the menu was–thus managing to repeat favorite dishes but not always for the same friends.

This chapter, more than any other in the book, is for "Us" whether BC or not. Of course, if you have children they are bound to want some the next day, but at least your efforts will not have been wasted if they don't like it.

For those special, relaxed evenings, here are some examples of dinner party menus. The recipes are mouth-watering, most of them can be prepared in advance and they can also be used for daytime gatherings–after all, without the children to consider, afternoons and evenings just roll into one.

DINNER PARTY ONE
serves four

This is an interesting menu, and most of the recipes can be prepared in advance. The Walnut and Cheese Pâté used to be a great favorite at our restaurant, and the Double Chocolate, Nut and Raisin Delight... Well, it's delicious.

Walnut and Cream Cheese Pâté with Warm Olive Bread

Normandy Galettes with Country Cider Sauce
Noodles with Spinach
Roasted Red Bell Peppers and Onions

Double Chocolate, Nut and Raisin Delight

DINNER PARTY TWO
serves four

Burritos as a main course make for an informal atmosphere over the table. Virtually anything goes with a burrito, so they are ideal for using up leftover cooked beans or vegetables. The Raspberry Cream Pots provide a light finish.

Chili Bean Soup with Nachos

Burritos with Fire Sauce and Salsa
Stir-fried Broccoli and Cashews
Herby Green Salad

Raspberry Cream Pots

DINNER PARTY THREE
serves four

This dinner party menu has a distinctly Oriental slant to it. I enjoy cooking Oriental food primarily, I suppose, because in most cases it's 95% preparation and only 5% cooking. The first cook I worked with at the restaurant Food For Thought was Siraporn from Thailand. Her thoughts on cooking have stayed with me ever since: keep food fresh and the flavors simple.

Thai Satay Soup

Shiitake and Tempeh Teriyaki Skewers with Dipping Sauce
Szechuan Braised Bell Peppers
Yellow Chinese Rice

Tropical Caramel Cream

DINNER PARTY FOUR
serves four

This dinner party has a distinctly Italian flavor. My love affair with warm salads continues. The menu combines two seemingly contrary techniques–Broiled Salad and Roasted Vegetable Lasagne. Both ideas work extremely well and will certainly surprise your guests.

Broiled Salad with Mustard and Sherry Vinaigrette

Milanese Roasted Vegetable Lasagne
Swiss Chard with Lime
Mushroom Crostini

Strawberry and Fresh Fig Brûlée

Overleaf Left-WALNUT AND CREAM CHEESE PÂTÉ WITH WARM OLIVE BREAD *Right*-NORMANDY GALETTES WITH COUNTRY CIDER SAUCE, NOODLES WITH SPINACH, ROASTED RED BELL PEPPERS AND ONIONS

Walnut and Cream Cheese Pâté

½ stick unsalted butter

4 shallots or small onions, finely chopped

1 teaspoon paprika

2 garlic cloves, crushed

1 teaspoon snipped fresh chives

1½ cups cottage cheese

½ cup sour cream

1 cup ricotta cheese

1 cup walnuts, lightly toasted and chopped

2 teaspoons Dijon mustard

2 teaspoons lemon juice

2 cups vegetarian mature Cheddar cheese, shredded

fine sea salt and freshly ground black pepper

TO DECORATE:

½ cup cream cheese

2 scallions, finely chopped

¼ cup walnut pieces, toasted

¼ cup black olives, pitted

This pâté was a great favorite at the restaurant. Uncannily meaty, it should be frozen if you want to keep it for more than a week.

1 Use a quarter of the butter to grease a loaf pan. In a small, heavy-bottom saucepan melt the rest of the butter and sauté the shallots until they begin to soften.

2 In a bowl or food processor beat the rest of the ingredients together, then fold in the shallots. Spoon the mixture into the greased loaf pan, spreading it evenly. Place in a preheated oven, 325°F, for 1 hour.

3 Remove the pâté from the oven and let cool. When cool the pâté must be refrigerated for a further 3 hours before it can be turned out of the pan onto a plate.

4 To decorate, beat the cream cheese with the scallions in a small bowl and season with salt and pepper to taste. Spread it over the pâté and decorate with walnuts and olives.

5 To serve, cut the pâté into slices and serve with a salad garnish, together with your favorite hot or toasted bread.

Olive Bread

2½ cups unbleached white bread flour

1 heaped teaspoon fine sea salt

¾ cake compressed yeast, or ½ teaspoon active dry yeast

1½ cups warm water

½ teaspoon soft brown sugar

1 tablespoon extra-virgin olive oil

10 black olives, pitted

3 garlic cloves, crushed (optional)

1 tablespoon chopped fresh rosemary, thyme or sage (optional)

3 tablespoons chopped sun-dried tomatoes and/or green olives (optional)

½ tablespoon coarse sea salt

extra-virgin olive oil, for drizzling

Olive bread is a delicious, moist, flat bread originally made in the hearths of Italian kitchens. It is commonly known as focaccia or schiacciata. Enriched with olive oil, focaccia will re-heat successfully and is a superb accompaniment to pâtés, soups and cheese.

1 Put the flour in a large bowl and mix in the fine sea salt. Crumble the fresh yeast into some of the warm water with the sugar in a jug or bowl, cover and let stand for 10 minutes until it starts to froth.

2 Make a well in the flour, add the yeast mixture and the oil and start to knead the dough, adding more water if necessary. The dough must be soft so make it on the sticky side. Place in a clean, warm, lightly oiled bowl and cover with a damp dishcloth. Let rise in a warm, draft-free place until doubled in bulk, 30-40 minutes.

3 Remove the dough from the bowl and place on a clean, lightly floured work surface. Knead in the olives and any of the other ingredients–garlic, herbs, sun-dried tomatoes or green olives–you wish to include. As you knead the dough, shape it into a ball. Place the ball of dough on a greased baking sheet, then spread it out with your fingers to form a round 12 inches in diameter and ½ an inch thick. Brush the surface with a little water and sprinkle with the coarse sea salt. Let it rise a second time in a warm place until it has doubled in size, then bake on the middle shelf of a pre-heated oven, 425°F, for about 20 minutes.

4 Remove from the oven and drizzle with extra-virgin olive oil and sprinkle on more sea salt, if you like. Focaccia is best eaten warm and may easily be re-heated in a hot oven for 5-10 minutes.

Normandy Galettes

1 tablespoon corn oil
1 onion, finely chopped
3 garlic cloves, crushed
1 tablespoon chopped fresh thyme
¾ cup celery, finely diced
¾ cup celeriac, shredded
2 cups zucchini, shredded
1 tablespoon shoyu
1 tablespoon whole grain mustard
2½ cups hot water, or use half water and
    half white wine
4 cups whole wheat bread crumbs
1⅛ cups cooked brown rice
2 free-range eggs, beaten (optional)
COATING:
2 eggs from free-range chickens, beaten
2 cups whole wheat bread crumbs
⅓ cup sesame seeds or regular oats
fine sea salt and freshly ground black pepper
oil, for shallow frying

"Galette" is a generic term for almost anything round, flat, edible and shallow fried. They are usually made out of potatoes or grains but can also resemble robust pancakes.

1 Heat the oil in a skillet. Add the onion, garlic and thyme and cook until the onion begins to soften. Add the celery, celeriac and zucchini and continue to cook for another 8 minutes.

2 Stir in the shoyu and mustard. Add the water, or water and wine, and bring to a boil, simmer for 3 minutes then remove from the heat.

3 Fold in the bread crumbs, rice and beaten egg, if using, and mix to a smooth consistency. Divide the mixture into 8 and roll into balls. With lightly floured hands, flatten each ball to form a galette about ½ an inch thick. Chill them for several hours or, if time permits, overnight, before moving on to the next stage.

4 For the coating, place the beaten egg in a shallow saucer. Mix together the bread crumbs, sesame seeds or oats, and seasoning and place in another saucer. Dip each galette in the beaten egg, then dip in the bread crumb mixture, coating thoroughly.

5 Shallow fry the galettes in hot oil in a large skillet until they are golden brown all over, about 5 minutes on each side. Serve hot with Country Cider Sauce (see page 22).

Country Cider Sauce

¼ stick butter

4 shallots, finely chopped

3½ tablespoons unbleached all-purpose white flour

3¾ cups hard cider

⅔ cup light cream

squeeze of lemon

¼ stick unsalted butter, chilled (optional)

fine sea salt and freshly ground black pepper

1 Melt the butter in a saucepan. Add the shallots and cook gently until they begin to soften. Stir in the flour and cook for 1 minute. Add the cider gradually, stirring all the time. Boil rapidly until the sauce thickens, then leave on a low heat to simmer.

2 Place the cream in a separate saucepan, heat gently to reduce by half, then gradually add the cider sauce.

3 Add a few drops of lemon juice, and, if you are not serving the sauce immediately, a few cubes of chilled unsalted butter. Adjust the seasoning to taste.

Noodles with Spinach

1 pound spinach, stalks removed

4 cups (12 ounces) dried tagliatelle

½ stick unsalted butter

1 onion, thinly sliced

3 garlic cloves, crushed

pinch of freshly shredded nutmeg

1 tablespoon lightly toasted bread crumbs

fine sea salt and freshly ground black pepper

I love noodles with spinach—any noodles will do and the spinach has to be fresh. They make a particularly pleasant accompaniment to anything that has been pan fried—try them and you will be converted, too! Buy firm fresh leaves which are bright in color and crisp in texture.

1 Wash the spinach in plenty of cold water, being careful not to leave it immersed, which will make it soggy. Just dip it in and out until you feel that it is clean.

2 Put a large saucepan of water on to boil and cook the pasta according to the instructions on the package. (The water should have a gently rolling boil when the pasta is added.)

3 Melt the butter in a deep saucepan, add the onion and sauté gently for 5-6 minutes. Add the garlic and spinach and cook for a further 4-5 minutes until the spinach is just cooked. Season to taste with nutmeg, salt and pepper.

4 When the pasta is cooked, drain it thoroughly, and fold into the spinach. Tip the pasta and spinach into a large serving dish and sprinkle with the lightly toasted bread crumbs. Serve at once.

Roasted Red Bell Peppers and Onions

4 red bell peppers, cored, seeded and quartered

4 small onions, peeled and halved

1 tablespoon extra-virgin olive oil

1 teaspoon dried thyme

fine sea salt and freshly ground black pepper

This side dish is so simple that you'll feel guilty that you haven't done any real work. The sad thing is that the peppers tend to disappear not only in the oven but as soon as they are served, so I suggest making a bit more than would normally seem necessary as there are never, ever, leftover roasted red peppers!

1 Brush a roasting pan with a little of the olive oil. Place the vegetables in the pan, then brush them with the remaining olive oil. Sprinkle with thyme, season, and place in a preheated oven, 400°F, for 20-30 minutes or until well roasted and soft.

2 Remove from the oven, transfer to a dish and serve. (I do not recommend removing the skins unless they are black.)

Double Chocolate, Nut and Raisin Delight

¼ cup brandy

3 tablespoons Cointreau or Triplesec

1 tablespoon Amaretto

1 tablespoon strong black coffee

3 cups (12 ounces) amaretti-sprinkled ladyfingers

2 cups heavy cream

1 cup confectioners' sugar

1 cup white chocolate, broken into pieces

½ cup Belgian dark chocolate, broken into pieces

½ cup nibbed almonds, toasted

½ cup nibbed hazelnuts, toasted

⅓ cup plump black raisins (soaked in
  brandy, if you like)

Here's a dessert that will certainly cause a stir–definitely one to save for the adults. You will need a 5 cup ovenproof bowl lined with damp cheesecloth.

I suggest using amaretti-sprinkled ladyfingers for the flavor if possible, but ordinary ladyfingers are fine, too.

1 Line a 5-cup ovenproof bowl with damp cheesecloth.

2 Mix the liqueurs and coffee together in a small bowl.

3 Use the ladyfingers to line the insides of the bowl, on top of the cheesecloth, making sure that they fit snugly and retaining enough ladyfingers for the top of the pudding. Soak the ladyfingers in two-thirds of the liqueur mixture, setting the remaining third to one side.

4 Whip the heavy cream with the confectioners' sugar until soft peaks form and divide into 2 separate bowls.

5 Place the white chocolate in a small heatproof bowl and place over a saucepan of gently simmering water. When melted and cooled, whisk the chocolate into the cream in one of the bowls until the mixture is very firm. Repeat for the dark chocolate.

6 Fold the nuts into the white chocolate mousse and then spread the mixture on the insides of the ladyfingers lining the bowl. Add the raisins to the dark chocolate mousse and pour this mixture into the center of the pudding.

7 Dip the remaining ladyfingers into the reserved liqueur mixture and place on top of the pudding. Cover with the cheesecloth, then place a saucer or small plate on top. Weight down and refrigerate for at least 12 hours.

8 To serve, remove the weight and saucer or plate. Turn the pudding out onto a serving plate, and remove the cheesecloth.

Chili Bean Soup with Nachos

3 tablespoons extra-virgin olive oil

1 red onion, chopped

3 garlic cloves, crushed

1 teaspoon ground cumin

1 fresh red chili, seeded and chopped

1 teaspoon dried basil

1 teaspoon dried oregano

½ tablespoon lime or lemon juice

½ tablespoon soft brown sugar

4 tablespoons tomato paste

2 x 8 ounce cans black kidney beans

1 tablespoon vegetarian Worcestershire sauce

1 tablespoon shoyu

4 cups vegetable stock

TOPPING:

2 x 8-inch corn tortillas, or ready-made
corn chips

oil, for frying

½ cup vegetarian mature Cheddar cheese, for serving

This hearty soup could easily turn into a main course if you're not careful. In addition to nachos, try adding sour cream, guacamole, salsa or even just chopped fresh cilantro. The soup is best made the day before eating it.

1 Heat the oil in a large heavy-bottom saucepan or casserole dish, add the onion, garlic, spices, chili and herbs and sauté together gently for 6 minutes. Add the remaining ingredients and bring to a boil. Then simmer for 25-30 minutes.

2 Remove half of the soup and purée it before returning it to the rest of the soup in the pan. (This is best done the day before.)

3 Cut each corn tortilla, if your're using, into 8 wedges and fry in a little oil until crisp. Alternatively, use ready-made corn chips.

4 To serve, pour the hot soup into individual ovenproof bowls.

Top with corn chips and cheese, and place under a broiler for a few minutes until the cheese is bubbling and golden brown. Serve at once.

Burritos with Fire Sauce and Salsa

8 x 8-inch flour tortillas (see page 128)

⅔ cup sour cream

1 tablespoon chopped fresh chives or mint

1 cup mozzarella cheese, shredded (optional)

¼ cup freshly shredded Parmesan cheese (optional)

fine sea salt and freshly ground black pepper

BURRITO FILLING:

3 tablespoons olive oil

1 onion, finely chopped

1 small eggplant, cut into ½-inch cubes

1 red bell pepper, cored, seeded and diced

¾ cup flat mushrooms, chopped

2 garlic cloves, crushed

½ cup nibbed almonds, toasted

8 ounce can corn, drained

1 cup vegetarian mature Cheddar cheese,
shredded (optional)

FIRE SAUCE:

1 tablespoon olive oil

1 onion, finely chopped

3 garlic cloves, crushed

2 teaspoons ground cumin

2 teaspoons dried oregano

2 fresh red chiles (seeded for a milder sauce)

¼ teaspoon ground coriander

1½ cups red wine

3 tablespoons tomato paste

2 x 8 ounce cans chopped tomatoes

1 teaspoon orange peel

SALSA:

1 red bell pepper, cored, seeded and halved

1 fresh jalapeño pepper, halved (seeded
   for a milder sauce)

extra-virgin olive oil, for brushing

2 ripe avocados

3 tablespoons lemon or lime juice

1 bunch of scallions, white parts only, chopped

3 teaspoons chopped cilantro, for garnish

If it's not a really special occasion, burritos are an ideal way of using up leftover cooked beans and vegetables—just about everything goes and like all good Mexican food you can bolt on as many extras as you feel happy with. Burritos are essentially anything wrapped up in a soft flour tortilla and baked.

For this recipe, simply warm the tortillas through in a microwave to loosen them up if necessary—this will make rolling them easier. Don't re-cook them. The filling can be made a day in advance, and the Fire Sauce is best made the day before eating. Chili sauces are very much a matter of personal taste so adjust the heat to your own preference.

The salsa is best made just before serving—everything can be prepared in advance except for the avocados.

1 To make the filling, heat the oil in a large saucepan or casserole dish. Add the onion and eggplant and cook gently for 5 minutes, stirring occasionally to prevent sticking or burning.

2 Stir in the red pepper, mushrooms and garlic. Cover and cook gently for 10 minutes before adding the almonds and corn. Season to taste.

3 Divide the mixture evenly between the 8 tortillas and top with cheese, if you're using, before rolling them up tightly into cylindrical shapes. Place in a lightly oiled baking dish.

4 For the fire sauce, heat the oil in a deep heavy-bottom saucepan. Add the onion, garlic, cumin, oregano, chiles and coriander. Cook until the onion begins to soften and darken in color. Turn up the heat and add the red wine. Simmer until reduced by half. Stir in the tomato paste followed by the chopped tomatoes. Bring to a boil then simmer for at least 30 minutes and up to 3 hours. Turn off the heat, season to taste and stir in the orange peel.

5 Meanwhile, stir the sour cream and spoon into a serving dish or individual ramekins. Season with a little coarse ground black pepper and a little chopped chives or mint.

6 To make the salsa, brush the red pepper and the jalapeño pepper with a little olive oil and roast in a preheated oven, 400°F, for about 15-20 minutes, until the skins begin to blister. Remove from the oven and let cool before chopping into small dice.

7 Halve the avocados, remove the pits and scoop out the flesh into a mixing bowl. Immediately beat in the lemon or lime juice to delay discoloration. Combine all the ingredients with a fork (not in a blender). Place in a serving dish or individual ramekins and sprinkle with chopped cilantro.

8 To assemble the burritos, pour the fire sauce around the burritos in their dish, trying to avoid splashing the tops. Sprinkle the tops with a little shredded mozzarella and Parmesan, if using.

9 Bake in a preheated oven, 325°F, until the cheese is melted, bubbling and brown, about 40 minutes.

10 Serve the burritos with the salsa and sour cream, preferably providing each guest with their own little ramekin of each.

Stir-fried Broccoli and Cashews

3 tablespoons oil

1½ pounds broccoli, cut into flowerets

1 medium carrot, cut into julienne strips

2 garlic cloves, crushed

¼ cup cashew nuts

1 bunch scallions, chopped

1 tablespoon shoyu

fine sea salt and freshly ground black pepper

Many vegetable dishes at dinner parties are precooked or pre-heated for ease. Occasionally you're given something fresh, something that takes a little time and effort at the last moment, but also something that is appreciated.

1 Heat the oil in a heavy skillet or wok. When the oil is very hot, add the broccoli and carrot and stir-fry for 3 minutes. Then add the garlic, cashews and scallions and stir-fry for about 4 minutes. Add the shoyu and let it reduce by half. Season to taste, cover and steam for 5 minutes.

Note. This dish is very versatile–I have kept it fairly bland as it is accompanying some pretty hot stuff! Other additions would be ginger, sherry, chili, spices and virtually any vegetable.

Herby Green Salad

1 gem lettuce

8 young spinach leaves

1 head of chicory

8 leaves of curly endive

8 leaves of rocket

1 tablespoon chopped fresh chervil

1 tablespoon chopped fresh mint

3 tablespoons torn basil leaves

1 tablespoon snipped fresh chives

DRESSING:

½ cup extra-virgin olive oil

5 tablespoons balsamic vinegar

fine sea salt and freshly ground black pepper

Giving recipes for salads always feels to me like telling someone how to make love. No doubt there are lots of tips that can be passed on. One tip, however, is to avoid using knives when preparing salad leaves.

1 Mix the leaves and herbs together in a large salad bowl. Combine the dressing ingredients and toss with the salad.

Raspberry Cream Pots

2 cups raspberries

4 tablespoons soft brown sugar

4 egg yolks

1¼ cups heavy cream

1½ tablespoons framboise or kirsch

sour cream, for decoration

After such a substantial and fairly spicy meal a light fruity dessert is required. This one has the added advantage of being able to be prepared hours beforehand.

1 Reserve a few raspberries for decoration and place the rest in a blender or food processor with the sugar and eggs. Blend together, then rub through a strainer into a bowl. Stir in the cream and framboise or kirsch; then pour into 4 individual ramekins.

2 Place the ramekins in an ovenproof dish or roasting pan containing enough hot water to cover two-thirds of the depth of the ramekins. Place in a preheated oven, 275°F, for at least 1 hour until the edges are set and the centers are slightly wobbly.

3 Let the pots cool, then chill for 6 hours.

4 To serve, top each ramekin with a dollop of sour cream and the reserved raspberries.

Thai Satay Soup

1 stalk of lemon grass, roughly chopped

6 shallots, roughly chopped

4 garlic cloves, crushed

1-inch piece of fresh ginger root, finely chopped

½ teaspoon ground turmeric

½ teaspoon chili powder

3 tablespoons lemon juice or tamarind sauce

3 tablespoons water

1 tablespoon sesame oil

3½ cups vegetable stock

2½ cups dried medium egg noodles

16 ounce can coconut milk

8 ounces firm tofu, cut into ½-inch cubes

2 cups bean sprouts

1 cup Chinese black mushrooms, sliced

fine sea salt and freshly ground black pepper

Siraporn would certainly have approved of this soup. It has clean lines and a clear distinctive flavor. Don't be put off by the longish list of ingredients, it's easy.

1 Blend the first 6 ingredients together in a bowl with 1 tablespoon of the lemon juice or tamarind sauce and the water to form a paste. Heat the sesame oil in a large, heavy-bottom saucepan. Stir into the paste, return this to the pan and cook for about 15 minutes. Add the vegetable stock, stir and bring to a boil, then simmer for another 15 minutes.

2 Meanwhile, in another saucepan, cook the noodles according to the instructions on the package.

3 Strain the soup into a clean pan and add the coconut milk. Add tofu, bean sprouts, and mushrooms and simmer for 3 minutes.

4 Drain the cooked noodles and add to the soup with the rest of the lemon juice or tamarind sauce. Season to taste with salt and pepper and serve the soup piping hot.

Shiitake and Tempeh Teriyaki Skewers

1 pound shiitake mushrooms

1 pound tempeh, cut into 1-inch cubes

corn oil, for shallow frying

1 tablespoon cilantro leaves, for garnish

MARINADE:

1 cup mirin

½ cup shoyu

3 tablespoons sesame oil

3 tablespoons lemon juice

1 tablespoon ginger juice, or shredded ginger root

BATTER:

1 egg

2 cups ice-cold water

pinch of baking soda

¾ cup unbleached all-purpose white flour

fine sea salt and freshly ground black pepper

DIPPING SAUCE:

½ cup light tahini (do not use dark, toasted tahini)

¼ cup cashew nut butter

½ cup barley miso

¾ cup marinade

2 garlic cloves, crushed

This recipe is a bit of a cheat on two counts. Although they can be broiled, the skewers are much better shallow fried and I prefer to use the dipping sauce as a sploshing sauce. In other words, I tend to pour it over the skewers to ensure even distribution. If you are a vegan, leave out the Tempura batter or substitute it with a pakora batter and deep-fry the skewers.

You will need 12 wooden skewers. Soak them in water before use to prevent them from burning.

Overleaf Left-THAI SATAY SOUP *Right*-SHIITAKE AND TEMPEH TERIYAKI SKEWERS, SZECHUAN BRAISED PEPPERS, YELLOW CHINESE RICE.

1 Mix the marinade ingredients in a clean, plastic container. Add the mushrooms and tempeh and let marinate in a cool place for at least 3 hours or overnight.

2 Remove the mushrooms and the tempeh from the marinade with a slotted spoon and let drain thoroughly on a wire rack before threading alternately onto the skewers.

3 Whisk the batter ingredients together until frothy. Tempura batter should be very thin. If it is at all thick add a little more iced water. Do not overbeat the batter.

4 When ready to eat, simply dip the skewers in the batter and shallow fry in hot corn oil. Keep warm in the oven.

5 The dipping sauce can be made as soon as the mushrooms and tempeh are removed from the marinade by stirring all the ingredients together until well combined.

Szechuan Braised Bell Peppers

4 large red, yellow or green bell peppers, cored,
  seeded and quartered
sesame oil, for brushing
a little vegetable oil, for oiling
½ quantity Teriyaki marinade (see Shiitake and
  Tempeh Teriyaki Skewers, page 27)
3 teaspoons brown sugar
6 scallions, finely sliced
4 tablespoons chopped cilantro
1 teaspoon hot chili sauce
¼ cup sesame seeds, toasted
fine sea salt

This is a very simple and tasty recipe that will add plenty of color and flavor to any meal. Eaten with the Shiitake and Tempeh Teriyaki Skewers (see page 27) it also conveniently uses up the rest of the marinade. Obviously, if you are not using the skewer recipe and are cooking these peppers as an accompaniment to another meal, you'll have to make up about half the quantity of the marinade used for the skewers.

1 Lightly brush the quarters of pepper with the sesame oil and place them on a lightly oiled baking sheet in a preheated oven, 400°F, and cook for about 30 minutes.

2 Meanwhile, mix the marinade with the rest of the ingredients, except the sesame seeds.

3 When the peppers are ready, cut into strips and toss in the dressing. Sprinkle with toasted sesame seeds and serve.

Yellow Chinese Rice

1 cup Basmati rice
¼ cup wild rice
a few saffron threads
1 tablespoon water
2-inch piece of lemon grass
4-5 tablespoons sesame oil
½ cup cashew nuts
1 large onion, shredded
2 garlic cloves, crushed
1 fresh green chili, finely sliced
1 cup bamboo shoots
¼ cup red pickled ginger
¾ cup green beans or sugar snaps,
  blanched thoroughly

Here's a delicious rice recipe that would make a meal on its own. Chinese and Japanese cooks tend to use short- or medium-grained rice to accompany their savory dishes but if you prefer, use a long-grain rice like Basmati. Red rice from the Camargue in France is a tasty addition and contrasts well with the yellow color, which is a feature of the saffron rice. If you can't get saffron use 1½ teaspoons turmeric instead, which will still give a good yellow coloring.

1 Thoroughly wash both rice separately under cold running water and then drain well. Soak the saffron threads in the measured

water for about 10-15 minutes and then set aside.

2 Cook the Basmati rice in a large saucepan of water with the saffron and the lemon grass for about 10-15 minutes until just tender. Drain well and cool. Cook the wild rice separately in boiling water until tender.

3 Heat 2 tablespoons of sesame oil in a large heavy-bottom skillet. Add the cashews and sauté until golden. Remove with a slotted spoon and set aside. Add the shredded onion, garlic and chili and cook for about 10 minutes over a reasonably high heat, stirring frequently to prevent burning. Pour in the rest of the sesame oil, heat, then stir in the remaining ingredients and both quantities of rice, mixing well.

4 If you're short of time for serving, the rice can be covered with foil and kept warm in an oven. Alternatively, cook it earlier in the day and re-heat it in a microwave oven before combining with the other ingredients.

5 Garnish the rice with the fried cashews and serve immediately. This dish is goes extremely well with the Szechuan Braised Bell Peppers and Shiitake and Tempeh Teriyaki Skewers (see pages 27-30).

Tropical Caramel Cream

1 ripe banana, thickly sliced

1 small ripe pineapple, cut into
   ½-inch cubes

1 small cantaloupe melon, cut into
   ½-inch cubes

2 passion fruit, halved

3 tablespoons Midori

3 tablespoons freshly squeezed orange juice

½ cup heavy cream

½ cup plain yogurt

¼ cup soft brown sugar

1 tablespoon water

After a fairly taxing appetizer and main course, it makes sense to have a simple dessert. If the rest of the food has been hot and spicy the ideal dessert will be cool, comforting and cleansing like this one. This dish is best served in large individual glasses or glass dessert bowls.

1 Divide the prepared fruit between 4 glass dessert bowls. Mix the Midori and orange juice together and pour over the fruit. (If preferred, substitute 1 tablespoon of rum for the aperitif and use 3 tablespoons of orange juice.)

2 Whip the cream until soft peaks form and fold in the plain yogurt. Spoon this mixture generously over the fruit.

3 Gently heat the sugar with the water in a small heavy-bottom saucepan until the sugar has dissolved. Boil rapidly until the syrup is golden. Set aside to darken in color.

4 Oil a large sheet of foil and pour the syrup over it in small and irregular shapes. Let cool. Peel off the caramel pieces and stick into the cream when you are ready to serve.

Milanese Roasted Vegetable Lasagne

12 sheets of lasagne, precooked in boiling water, then
    drained and cooled
sliced tomatoes, for garnish

MILANESE TOMATO SAUCE:

1½ tablespoons olive oil
1 onion, chopped
4 garlic cloves, crushed
1 green bell pepper, cored, seeded and diced
1½ cups field mushrooms (porcini if possible), chopped
8 basil leaves, torn into pieces
2 teaspoons dried oregano
1 bay leaf
¾ cup full-bodied red wine
3 tablespoons tomato paste
2 x 8 ounce cans chopped tomatoes
8 ounces tomatoes, peeled, seeded
    and chopped

FILLING:

3 tablespoons extra-virgin olive oil
1 large eggplant, quartered
2 large zucchini, quartered
1 large red pepper, cored, seeded and quartered
1 large yellow pepper cored, seeded and quartered
1 fennel bulb, quartered
4 shallots or small onions, halved
1 tablespoon dried thyme or similar herb
fine sea salt and freshly ground black pepper

CHEESE SAUCE:

2½ cups milk
¾ stick butter
½ cup unbleached all-purpose white flour
1 egg yolk (optional)
½ cup Gorgonzola, dolcelatte or Stilton

cheese, shredded
½ cup mature vegetarian Cheddar cheese, shredded
½ mozzarella cheese, shredded
½ teaspoon cayenne pepper
3 tablespoons sour cream (optional)
fine sea salt and freshly ground black pepper

In recent years I seem to be increasingly roasting or broiling vegetables basted with olive oil, and perhaps seasoned or sprinkled with herbs. For a start, I love the flavor that develops; secondly, the texture of the vegetables changes wonderfully and, thirdly, the individual vegetables seem to retain more of their own identity than if they had been stir-fried together. My favorite vegetables for roasting, apart from the traditional ones, are eggplants, bell peppers, zucchini, tomatoes, onions, fennel, garlic and shallots. The technique is very simple and well worth experimenting with.

All sorts of lasagne are available these days. If you can't get or make fresh lasagne, buy the type that requires boiling. "No precooking" lasagne is a bit of a risk as it tends to absorb water from your sauce, making the dish a little dry. You can compensate by making runnier sauces but I find this a bit hit and miss. Try to make the Tomato Sauce the day before, as it improves with age.

1 Make the tomato sauce well in advance. Heat the oil in a pan, sauté the onion until soft, then add the rest of the vegetables and herbs and cook for another 5 minutes. Add the wine and cook gently to reduce by half. Stir in the tomato paste, quickly followed by the canned and fresh tomatoes. Bring to a boil, then gently simmer for at least 1 hour (2 hours would be better). Set the sauce aside to cool, then refrigerate.

2 The filling is simple to make. Brush a baking sheet with olive oil; brush each piece of vegetable with oil and arrange on the baking sheet. Season with dried herbs, salt and pepper. Roast in a preheated oven, 400°F, until cooked, about 40-60 minutes. Set aside to cool. When cool you may wish to cut the vegetables further–I prefer them chunky myself.

3 Make the cheese sauce by warming the milk in a large heavy-bottom saucepan. Melt the butter in another saucepan, add the

flour, and cook for a few minutes without letting it color. Then gradually add the warmed milk, stirring constantly to keep the mixture smooth. When all the milk has been added let the sauce simmer very gently for about 10 minutes. Stir in the egg yolk, if using, cheeses and seasoning, and remove from the heat. Add the sour cream and adjust the seasoning, if necessary.

4 To assemble the lasagne, brush the bottom of a 10 cup oven-proof dish generously with olive oil. Place 4 sheets of lasagne on the bottom of the dish and top with half of the tomato sauce, half of the roasted vegetables and one-third of the cheese sauce. Top this with 4 more sheets of lasagne and repeat the process until you have one-third of the cheese sauce left, with which to top the remaining layer of lasagne. Garnish with the tomato slices.

5 Place in a preheated oven, 350°F, and bake for about 45-55 minutes, or until the top is golden. Allow the lasagne to stand for 10 minutes before serving with the broiled salad and Swiss chard.

Broiled Salad with Mustard and Sherry Vinaigrette

1 head of chicory, pulled apart
12 leaves of rocket, or 1 head of gem lettuce
¾ cup fresh sun-ripened tomatoes, peeled, seeded and
    diced
¼ cup sun-dried tomatoes, chopped
2 radicchio, cut into 8 wedges
½ cup walnut pieces
1 cup goat's cheese, crumbled, or
    ½ cup freshly shredded Parmesan cheese
    (both optional)
fine sea salt and freshly ground black pepper
VINAIGRETTE:
3 garlic cloves, crushed
1 tablespoon whole grain mustard

3 tablespoons sherry vinegar
½ cup extra-virgin olive oil
1 tablespoon chopped fresh parsley
1 tablespoon snipped fresh chives
1 teaspoon chopped fresh tarragon
fine sea salt and freshly ground black pepper

If you are short of time and ingredients for this salad, the radicchio broiled on its own with the vinaigrette is a wonderful treat.
1 Make the vinaigrette dressing well in advance. Allow the flavors to mingle by combining the ingredients thoroughly.
2 Mix together the chicory, rocket or lettuce, and tomatoes in a salad bowl.
3 Toss the radicchio in half of the vinaigrette dressing and pop it under a preheated broiler with the walnuts, until it browns around the edges.
4 Add to the rest of the salad and sprinkle with the remaining vinaigrette and cheese. Season to taste and serve.

Swiss Chard with Lime

1¾ pounds Swiss chard, or 1¼ pounds raw spinach
juice of 1 fresh lime
5 tablespoons extra-virgin olive oil
fine sea salt and freshly ground black pepper

Quick and simple, this is a delicious accompaniment to something rich like the Roasted Vegetable Lasagne. Much as I love spinach, given the choice I would always choose chard. For some reason it is usually fresher and more flavorsome.

Remove the large central spine with a sharp knife and cook it separately or save it for a stir-fried dish the next day.
1 Prepare the chard or spinach. Tear the larger leaves apart and wash thoroughly. Chard leaves can be a bit gritty but, unlike spinach, will not wilt so readily in water.

2 Mix the lime juice with 4 tablespoons of olive oil and season with salt and pepper.

3 In a saucepan, heat the remaining olive oil, add the chard, and stir. Cover and let cook for 5 minutes over a medium heat, then remove the lid. The chard should be almost cooked. Give it a stir and replace the lid for 1 minute more.

4 Just before serving, stir in the lime and oil, mixing well.

Mushroom Crostini

½ cup extra-virgin olive oil

1 large baguette or French bread, cut diagonally
   into about 16 slices

3 tablespoons chopped cilantro

3 garlic cloves, crushed

½ stick unsalted butter

2 cups fresh ceps or cup mushrooms

¼ cup dry white wine

¼ cup freshly shredded Parmesan
   cheese (optional)

fine sea salt and freshly ground black pepper

This is a good alternative to more mundane garlic bread. If you can get them, use fresh ceps instead of, or as well as, the fresh mushrooms. They are a delicious topping for crostini.

1 Use 7 tablespoons of the olive oil for brushing: brush a baking sheet with the oil and brush both sides of each baguette slice with olive oil. Arrange the slices on the baking sheet and place under a preheated broiler. Brown both sides carefully–try not to overcook them, as they burn easily. Remove and cool.

2 Mix the cilantro and garlic. Melt the butter and the remaining olive oil in a skillet. Add the mushrooms and sauté for 3 minutes. Add the wine and cook gently to reduce it by half. Lower the heat and stir in the chopped cilantro and garlic and season. Continue to cook gently for about 2 minutes more.

3 Remove from the heat, let cool and chop the mushrooms. Stir in Parmesan, if using, and set aside until ready to use.

5 Crostini are good served cold but even better warmed. Spoon some of the mushroom mixture onto each slice, then heat in the oven until the Parmesan has melted. Serve immediately.

Strawberry and Fresh Fig Brûlée

1 cup very ripe figs, sliced

1 cup strawberries, halved, or whole
   wild strawberries

1 vanilla pod, split lengthways

⅔ cup heavy cream

⅔ cup sour cream

4 egg yolks (small size eggs)

1 tablespoon fructose (fruit sugar)

soft brown sugar, for sprinkling

After a substantial main course, a light and fruity dessert is required. This variation of an old standard is always popular, so it's probably best to double the recipe and make 8 servings. Only use figs if they are perfectly ripe–if you can't get ripe figs use blackberries, blueberries or passion fruit.

1 Pile the fruit into and around the edges of 4 ramekin dishes. Place the vanilla pod in a pan. Stir in the two creams and heat to just below boiling point. Remove the pod.

2 Beat the egg yolks and fructose together in a pan, then gradually beat in the hot vanilla cream. Heat gently until the sauce has thickened. Pour the custard over the fruit in the ramekins and set aside to cool. When cool, chill for 2-3 hours until set.

3 Sprinkle the puddings with a little soft brown sugar and broil under a preheated hot broiler. The sugar should caramelize and, when allowed to cool, form a hard protective coating to the top of the custard cream and serve cold.

AND BABY MAKES THREE

Cooking is an act of love and caring. Some believe that the "kiss"–seemingly only associated with humans–originated as an expression of love. In the act of weaning their children, early female *Homosapiens* passed masticated food from their mouths directly into their children's mouths. There were many benefits attributed to this technique. Not only did the children start eating solids in a semi-liquid form, but the food was also much easier and safer to digest because it was mixed with the mother's saliva–a natural disinfectant and digestive. As the children grew older, feeding and then hunting and gathering food for themselves, this tender act was outgrown. Nowadays we have the food processor, the strainer and the hand-blender instead (I wonder what future anthropologists will make of them!). The "kiss" does remain, however; the touching of two people's lips as the ultimate expression of human love, caring, and kindness.

Before I go any further I feel that I should explain my qualifications in this subject. I am the father of three children–Daisy, twelve, Hamish, nine, and Mollie, three years old. Not unnaturally, all three have been brought up on a vegetarian diet, simply because their mother, Kate, is a vegetarian. Later in life they can make their own decisions but right now they eat what we eat at home, which is vegetarian food. I might add that Daisy, Hamish and Mollie are all of average height and intelligence. They have never suffered from anything more than the common cold; they don't suffer from flatulence; they look lovely, healthy, and vibrant and they all enjoy sports. What is more, they have never really had any health additives apart from those extra vitamins which mysteriously appear in cereal packets. In fact, Hamish and Mollie have both been sick, related to food, once in their lives. Modern food pundits would expect our children to be sullen, thick, pale, physical wrecks, racked with lethargy and not nice to be in a confined space with. I am going to make a rather sensational statement now–it is not in my nature but I'm going to do it all the same: I think that all healthy women, during pregnancy and while nursing, should be vegetarian and, equally, babies should be weaned onto pure vegetarian food, ideally organic foods, that have as few chemicals in or on them as possible. Why? Because it seems to me that the common problems associated with pregnancy and feeding after birth are diet or health related. Smoking, should be taboo but there's nothing much wrong with the odd glass of wine in the later stages–as a morale booster it could also be very beneficial. A good well-balanced vegetarian (not vegan) diet is what most babies should be made from. Daisy, Hamish and Mollie are, I believe, the best evidence of this. Meat is an outdated form of protein that is over-farmed and overpriced and if you want to be overweight, too, then carry on eating it, especially when you are pregnant.

It's all simple really: You are what you eat. In this chapter we will be looking at the four phases of feeding a baby. First during pregnancy before the baby is born; then the first 6 months when he or she will be primarily nursed or formula fed; then 6-12 months when more and more solids will be introduced and lastly from 12 months onward, when effectively the baby will want to share in family meals.

DURING PREGNANCY

So you're pregnant. I'm afraid I cannot speak from experience so these are the thoughts of my wife, Kate.

Everyone is different so it's best to speak broadly. The biggest misconception is to assume that because you are only just pregnant that somehow the effect on your body is less than when you're about to give birth. If anything, the reverse is true. The moment you conceive, your whole body starts to change. Even though the fetus is still microscopic it has a huge effect on you. Often the first change you experience is in your feelings toward food–for some women the mere thought of food makes them feel queasy. When I see relevant books on the subject recommending foods such as liver, kidney, oily fish, and smoked fish, I wonder if the authors have ever been pregnant themselves, or at least known anyone who has experienced pregnancy. No doubt at the beginning of your pregnancy you will be happiest with plain foods but as your pregnancy develops you may start to desire strange combinations. Toward the end you eat only what you can squeeze into your distended stomach and drink what your flattened bladder allows.

As a healthy vegetarian there is absolutely no problem in obtaining all of the goodness you need to develop a healthy baby, but some foods must definitely be avoided. These include raw or undercooked eggs, which may result in salmonella poisoning, and soft cheeses that are at risk from contamination by *listeria*. Generally though, vegetarians do not have as many problems with "risky" food as those who eat meat and fish. Too much fat will be a problem whether you are pregnant or not, but once again vegetarians tend to benefit here.

During an average week you will want to eat meals that include eggs, milk, cheese (mild vegetarian Cheddar at first), yogurt, seeds, pasta, cereals, beans, pulses, fresh vegetables, fresh fruit, nuts, and cold-pressed oils. Fresh fruit will be a constant source of refreshment to your taste buds and, of course, are excellent providers of vitamin C. Do wash all raw fruit and vegetables thoroughly before use, though, because any residual chemical sprays will go straight into your baby. Alternatively, buy good-quality organic produce.

Funnily enough, as you and your baby grow you will get over the initial shock to your body and despite the constant changing in your dimensions, things will seem more normal. As you become adjusted to your new state so your taste buds will return, sometimes with a vengeance. From about 3-7 months your eating habits will return to somewhere near normal, with perhaps an extra couple of nutritious snacks fitted in here and there. You might also find that you cannot eat a meal late in the evening, as your body takes longer to digest food, so rich food at a dinner party where the meal begins at 9:30 or 10 pm is not to be encouraged.

It is, of course, important for the baby that you steadily increase your weight by at least 18-20 pounds during the course of the pregnancy.

THE EARLY MONTHS

Here is a plain and wholesome menu to comfort you in those early and perhaps nauseous months of pregnancy. Use it as a dinner party or select component parts for meals on their own.

SERVES 4

Creamy Onion and Thyme Flan

Pasta Panzanella

Spring Salad

Strawberry and Banana Chocolate Truffle Pavlova

Date and Nut Loaf

Creamy Onion and Thyme Quiche

PIE DOUGH:

¾ cup organic whole wheat flour

¾ cup unbleached all-purpose white flour

2 teaspoons chopped fresh thyme

⅓ cup unsalted butter

2-3 tablespoons ice-cold water

FILLING:

2 Spanish onions, quartered

1 red bell pepper, cored, seeded and quartered

1 tablespoon extra-virgin olive oil

3 egg yolks from free-range chickens

⅔ cup light cream

⅔ cup whole milk

½ teaspoon freshly ground nutmeg

¾ cup Gruyère cheese, shredded

fine sea salt and freshly ground black pepper

sprigs of thyme, for garnish

Quiches are what real men don't eat! A good quiche is delicious hot or cold and ideal as an appetizer.

1 Mix the flours and the thyme in a cold bowl. Rub in the butter with your fingertips until the mixture resembles fine bread crumbs. Add enough of the cold water to mix to a smooth dough. Knead briefly before allowing the dough to chill for 30-60 minutes before rolling out.

2 Roll out the dough on a lightly floured surface and use to line a well-oiled 9-inch pie pan. If possible, freeze the pie shell at this stage–frozen pie shells can be cooked from frozen without the use of baking beans. If you don't have time for this, line the pie shell with wax paper and half fill it with ceramic beans. Bake for 10 minutes in a preheated oven, 400°F. Remove the beans and cook for another 5 minutes. If baking the pie shell from frozen, simply put it straight into the oven and cook for 10 minutes.

3 Meanwhile, brush the onions and the pepper with olive oil, place in a roasting pan and roast in the oven for 20-30 minutes until soft and lightly colored. When cooled, slice the onions and cut the pepper quarters into strips.

4 Beat the egg yolks, cream, milk, and nutmeg in a bowl and season with salt and pepper. Line the par-cooked pie shell with the onions. Top with the egg mixture, the cheese

Overleaf Left–CREAMY ONION AND THYME QUICHE, PASTA PANZANELLA *Right*–SPRING SALAD, STRAWBERRY AND BANANA CHOCOLATE TRUFFLE PAVLOVA

and decorate with the pepper strips and a few sprigs of fresh thyme.

5 Reduce the oven temperature to 350°F, and bake for 40 minutes, or until set and golden.

6 Serve the quiche as an appetizer with a salad garnish. Make individual quiches for slightly more special occasions.

Variation:
Replace the Spanish onions with shallots, mushrooms, peppers or tomatoes or all four.

Pasta Panzanella

6 cups of your favorite dried pasta

4 tablespoons dry white or brown bread crumbs, toasted until golden

2 tablespoons freshly shredded Parmesan cheese (optional)

2 tablespoons pine nuts, lightly toasted

2 tablespoons extra-virgin olive oil

2 red onions, chopped

4 garlic cloves, crushed

1 bunch of basil, torn into pieces

3 tablespoons sun-dried tomato paste, or ordinary tomato paste plus a few chopped sun-dried tomatoes

1 cup white wine

fine sea salt and freshly ground black pepper

When pregnant, standing over a hot stove is most uncomfortable. This rustic Italian pasta dish is quick to make, yet satisfying. Allow 1½ cups dried pasta per person.

1 Bring a large saucepan of lightly salted water to a boil and cook the pasta for 12 minutes or according to the package instructions, until firm to the bite.

2 Meanwhile, mix together the bread crumbs, Parmesan

and toasted pine nuts.

3 Heat the oil in a small saucepan and gently cook the chopped onions and garlic until beginning to soften. Add the basil and cook briefly before stirring in the tomato paste. When bubbling gently, add the white wine, stir well, and then bring back to a simmer. Season well.

4 Pour the sauce over the pasta and serve with a good sprinkling of the bread crumb mixture.

Variation:
Add more vegetables to the sauce, such as mushrooms, peppers, tomatoes or roasted eggplants.

Spring Salad

⅓ cup ripe black olives, pitted

4 pieces of sun-dried peppers in olive oil

1 carrot, cut into matchsticks, or 4 whole baby carrots

½ fennel bulb, thinly sliced

½ red or Spanish onion, thinly sliced

mixture of rocket and romaine lettuce

½ cup goat's cheese, for sprinkling (optional)

DRESSING:

1 tablespoon red wine vinegar

1 teaspoon Dijon mustard

5 tablespoons sun-dried pepper oil or extra-virgin olive oil

fine sea salt and freshly ground black pepper

This salad is a nice clean and light accompaniment to pasta, quick to prepare and tasty to eat.

1 Combine all the ingredients except the cheese and arrange in a large salad bowl or on individual plates.

2 Shake the dressing ingredients together in a screw-top jar to form an emulsion. Dress the salad when ready to serve and sprinkle with cheese, if you're using. Serve with chunks of fresh bread, such as ciabatta.

Strawberry and Banana Chocolate Truffle Pavlova

4 egg whites (large size) from free-range chickens

pinch of salt

1 cup soft brown sugar

1 teaspoon cornstarch

1 teaspoon vanilla extract

1 teaspoon lemon juice

½ cup plain Belgian chocolate or good quality real
    semisweet chocolate, broken into pieces

1 cup heavy cream

2 tablespoons cocoa powder

1 cup fresh ripe strawberries

2 bananas, sliced and tossed in lemon juice to
    prevent discoloration

This recipe certainly satisfies any cravings for chocolate and feeds hungry friends at the same time. If you're following the suggested menu this dish will use up the egg whites left over from the quiche.

Make the chocolate cream and decorate the pavlova literally within 1 hour of eating to avoid the meringue becoming soggy.

1 Line a baking sheet with greased wax paper.

2 Whisk the egg whites in a grease-free bowl with the salt until firm. Beat in the sugar, a tablespoon at a time, and continue beating until the mixture is very stiff. Fold in the cornstarch, vanilla extract and lemon juice.

3 Pour the mixture on to the wax paper and, using a spatula, spread the meringue mixture into a rough circle about 1½ inches thick. Bake for about 1 hour in a preheated oven, 275°F, then turn off the oven and leave the meringue to finish cooking and cool down in the closed oven. Allow at least 3 hours before eating at this stage.

4 Melt the chocolate in a heatproof bowl set over a saucepan of gently simmering water and then allow to cool slightly.

5 Whip the cream in a clean bowl until soft peaks form, then add half of the melted chocolate, whipping all the time. Beat in the remaining chocolate gently until the mixture is an even color. Spread the chocolate cream over the meringue and dust with the cocoa powder. Refrigerate for no more than 30 minutes.

6 Decorate the pavlova with the strawberries and bananas or other fruits in season and serve.

Date and Nut Loaf

a little oil, for oiling

1 cup boiling water

1¼ cup pitted dates

1 teaspoon baking soda

1 cup soft brown sugar

⅓ cup unsalted butter or vegan margarine

2½ cups organic whole wheat flour

1 teaspoon baking powder

½ teaspoon salt

½ cup chopped mixed nuts (choose your favorite)

1 Grease a loaf pan and line with greased wax paper. Mix the boiling water, the dates and the baking soda together in a bowl and leave to stand for 5 minutes.

2 Beat the sugar and butter until fluffy and stir in the date mixture. Sift the flour, baking powder and salt (retaining the bran) into the mixture and fold in the mixed nuts.

3 Turn the mixture into the loaf pan, smooth the top and bake in a preheated oven, 350°F, for 1 hour.

4 Turn out and cool on a wire rack. Serve with butter.

MID-TERM PREGNANCY

At this stage you will find that you will not want to stand on your feet for too long. Here are a couple of good, healthy, satisfying meals for you and your family or friends which are simple and quick to prepare.

Serves 4

Linguini and Spinach with Herby Walnut and Sun-Dried Tomato Pesto

Jolly Roger's Tipsy Cake

Linguini and Spinach with Herby Walnut and Sun-Dried Tomato Pesto

6 cups dried linguini, tagliatelle or spaghetti

2 tablespoons butter

3 tablespoons olive oil

2 large onions, finely sliced

4 garlic cloves, crushed

½ teaspoon chili powder

1½ cups chestnut mushrooms

1 pound fresh spinach

1 tablespoon tomato paste

fine sea salt and freshly ground black pepper

PESTO:

3 tablespoons finely chopped fresh parsley

3 tablespoons torn basil leaves

2 tablespoons chopped fresh mint

3 garlic cloves, crushed

grated peel and juice of 1 lemon

4 tablespoons finely chopped walnuts

3 tablespoons Parmesan cheese, freshly shredded

½ cup extra-virgin olive oil or sun-dried tomato oil

6 pieces of sun-dried tomatoes

The pasta you can prepare in advance; the pesto must be prepared in advance, but the spinach must be cooked just before serving. However, the spinach can be prepared beforehand–washed and any large stalks or brown leaves discarded. Choose healthy, alive-looking spinach, free from any blemishes.

1 Make the pesto by combining all the ingredients in a food processor or blender. Use the "pulse" action rather than "blend" to ensure that the ingredients are combined gradually to form a paste, not a purée. When prepared, set aside in a cool place–not the refrigerator unless you are storing it overnight–to allow the flavors a chance to develop.

2 Bring a large saucepan of lightly salted water to a boil. Cook the pasta according to the package instructions.

3 Meanwhile, melt the butter with the olive oil in a deep, heavy-bottom saucepan. Add the onions, garlic and chili powder. Cover and cook gently for 5 minutes. Stir in the mushrooms and cook for another 5 minutes.

4 When the mushrooms and onions have softened stir in the spinach, cook for a further 2 minutes and then add the tomato purée. Season to taste. Continue to cook for another 2 minutes. Remove from the heat and keep covered while the pasta finishes cooking.

5 Drain the pasta and toss immediately in the pesto. Serve topped with the spinach and more Parmesan, if you like.

Jolly Roger's Tipsy Cake

¾ cup sweet, dark fruit cake, broken into pieces

¼ cup crystallized ginger

4 large oranges, peeled, segmented and juice retained

grated peel and juice of 1 large lemon

4 tablespoons Madeira

3 tablespoons clear honey

1 cup heavy cream

2 egg whites

fruit, for decoration, such as strawberries,
    raspberries, kiwi fruit

*This is one of those desserts you simply can't fail with. It is easy
to make and delicious to eat. If you don't like store-bought cake,
make it yourself. The ingredients seem to give it the feel of piracy
on the Spanish Maine.*

1 Place the cake pieces in an attractive serving bowl. Top with
the ginger and oranges. (If, like me, you enjoy Madeira, splosh
some on top here also and perhaps trickle on some ginger syrup.)

2 Mix together the lemon peel and juice, Madeira and honey in a
small bowl.

3 In another bowl, whip the cream until soft peaks form, then
beat in the liquid, a little at a time, making sure that the cream
retains its shape.

4 Whisk the egg whites in a clean, grease-free bowl until soft
peaks form, then fold into the cream. Pour on top of the ginger
cake and chill for at least 2 hours before serving, decorated with
your chosen fruits.

Serves 4

Warm New Potato Salad

Red Pepper and Eggplant Pie with Mushroom Ragoût

Garden Salad with Orange Vinaigrette

Gooey Chewy Chocolate Brownies and Cream

Warm New Potato Salad

1 pound new potatoes

2 bunches of scallions, chopped

¾ cup vegetarian cheese, crumbled (optional)

DRESSING:

3 tablespoons white wine vinegar

1 tablespoon whole grain mustard

¼ cup extra-virgin olive oil

2 garlic cloves, crushed (optional)

1 teaspoon soft brown sugar

fine sea salt and freshly ground black pepper

*A nice way to serve tiny, sweet, and succulent new potatoes,
although it's equally good with regular potatoes–just double the
dressing to allow for absorption.*

1 Cook the potatoes in a saucepan of salted boiling water for 15
minutes or until tender.

2 Meanwhile, make the dressing by shaking all the ingredients
together in a jar with a lid.

3 When the potatoes are cooked, drain, mix with the spring
onions, and toss immediately in the dressing. Sprinkle the cheese
over the top, if using, and serve. The salad is best eaten straight-
away but is also tasty when eaten cold.

Overleaf Left–GARDEN SALAD WITH ORANGE VINAIGRETTE
Right–RED PEPPER AND EGGPLANT PIE, WARM POTATO SALAD

Red Bell Pepper and Eggplant Pie

3 large red bell peppers, cored, seeded and halved

2 large eggplants, trimmed and quartered

2 teaspoons dried oregano

3 tablespoons extra-virgin olive oil, plus
    extra for brushing

1 large onion, finely chopped

½ cup pine nuts

4 large ripe tomatoes, peeled, seeded and chopped,
    the juice retained

1 tablespoon tomato paste

2 tablespoons chopped fresh basil

pinch of freshly ground nutmeg

1 pound frozen puff pastry (2 packages), thawed

1 cup vegetarian cheese, crumbled

1 egg, beaten

3 tablespoons sesame seeds

fine sea salt and freshly ground black pepper

sprigs of mint and parsley, for garnish

RAGOÛT:

⅓ cup butter or 3 tablespoons olive oil

2 shallots, finely chopped

3 garlic cloves, crushed

1 teaspoon paprika

2 cups shiitake mushrooms, roughly chopped

2 cups chestnut mushrooms, roughly chopped

2 cups oyster mushrooms, roughly chopped

½ cup dry white wine

1 cup heavy cream (optional)

3 tablespoons chopped fresh parsley

This dish is extremely satisfying, best made in the summer when the ingredients are at their best, although they are usually available all year round.

1 Brush the peppers and eggplants with olive oil, place them on a baking sheet. Season them and sprinkle with oregano. Roast them in a preheated oven, 425°F, for 10 minutes, then add the pine nuts and continue roasting for another 5 minutes. Remove from the oven and allow to cool, then roughly chop the peppers and eggplants–they should not be quite cooked at this stage.

2 Heat the olive oil in a large pan, add the onion and cook for 5 minutes. Add the eggplants, peppers and pine nuts. Cook for 1 minute before stirring in the tomatoes. Bring the mixture quickly to a boil, stirring frequently to avoid burning. Add the tomato paste and cook for 1 minute. Finally, add the basil, nutmeg and seasoning and set aside to cool.

3 Roll out the puff pastry on a lightly floured cold surface to form a 12-inch square. Spoon the vegetable filling into the center, leaving a border 2 inches wide. Top with the crumbled cheese. With a knife, cut diagonal strips, 1½ inches long, down each side of the mixture. Tuck the ends over to form a plait.

4 Transfer the pie to a greased baking sheet, brush with beaten egg and sprinkle with sesame seeds. Allow to rest for 30 minutes in the refrigerator before baking.

5 Bake in a preheated oven, 425°F, for 15 minutes, then reduce the temperature to 375°F for at least another 15 minutes or until golden brown and risen.

6 To make the sauce, melt 3 tablespoons of the butter or 1 tablespoon of the oil in a pan. Add the shallots, garlic, and paprika and cook until beginning to soften. Stir in the shiitake and chestnut mushrooms and cook for 2 minutes.

7 Add the remaining butter or olive oil and when hot stir in the oyster mushrooms. Cook for 2 minutes and when the mixture is very hot add the wine and reduce by two thirds.

8 Pour in the cream, if you're using, and gently bring to a boil. Allow it to bubble away until reduced by half and thickened to a coating consistency. The sauce is now ready, so stir in the parsley and serve with the pie.

Garden Salad with Orange Vinaigrette

1½ cups fresh peas

4 bunches of watercress, stalks removed

1 orange, peeled and segmented

20 fresh mint leaves, finely chopped

DRESSING:

3 tablespoons freshly squeezed orange juice

1 tablespoon lemon juice

shredded peel of 2 oranges

pinch of sugar (optional)

4 tablespoons walnut oil

¼ cup safflower oil

fine sea salt and freshly ground black pepper

This is a really racy, fresh, and vibrant salad to rejuvenate your taste buds and is an excellent accompaniment to new potatoes in any meal. If fresh peas are unavailable, use frozen petit pois, snow peas, sugar snap peas, or fresh green beans or even barely cooked asparagus tips.

1 Cook the peas in a saucepan of salted boiling water for a few minutes. Drain well and mix with the watercress and orange segments; seasoning to taste. Arrange in a salad bowl.

2 Make the dressing by shaking all the ingredients together in a jar with a lid. Dress the salad liberally just before serving.

Gooey Chewy Chocolate Brownies

a little oil, for oiling

2⅛ cups (1¼ pounds) semisweet chocolate, broken into pieces

1 cup unsalted butter, diced

3 tablespoons fresh, strong coffee

¾ cup soft brown or white sugar

3 eggs from free-range chickens, beaten

¾ cup unbleached all-purpose white flour

1 teaspoon baking powder

½ teaspoon fine sea salt

1 cup raisins, or half raisins and half walnuts

1 teaspoon vanilla extract

This excellent recipe will serve you throughout your life; you'll use it time and time again for all your family and friends.

The brownies are good hot or cold for a main meal or as a snack. Remember, any brownie is only as good as the chocolate you use. Good chocolate contains nothing less than 35% cocoa solids—if you can, buy 70% cocoa solids—the flavor is truly remarkable.

1 Grease and line an 8 x 11-inch baking tray.

2 Melt the chocolate and butter in a heatproof bowl over a saucepan of gently boiling water.

3 While the coffee is hot, add the sugar to it, making sure it dissolves. When cool beat in the eggs.

4 Combine the remaining ingredients together in a bowl. Add the melted chocolate to the egg mixture and combine together well. Fold into the dry ingredients.

5 Pour into the prepared pan and bake in a preheated oven, 375°F, for about 45 minutes or until just firm to the touch.

6 Cut into squares and serve warm with cream and/or hot chocolate sauce.

TEN-MINUTE MEALS FOR
HEAVILY PREGNANT WOMEN

When you are huge–and this can happen at any time from 7 months onward–the last thing you will want to do is spend hours over a hot stove. The key words here are "speed," "simplicity" and "single pan"–you don't want to spend hours washing up, either! If you are cooking just for yourself then the quantities will be small, too, as you'll probably want six small meals throughout the day, rather than three larger ones.

The recipes given are all for four people but you may well find yourself cooking one tasty dish and saving the remainder for future meals. It is highly unlikely that you will attempt to cook desserts but will prefer cut-up fruits, and yogurts instead, plus, of course, the occasional square or, more likely, bar of pure chocolate.

In the month or two before giving birth meals must remain highly nutritious and quality, not quantity, is most important. Here are five small, tasty, and healthy meals suitable for a day in late-term pregnancy.

Chinese Noodles, Peppers and Tofu

3 cups Chinese egg noodles

1 tablespoon sesame oil

4 scallions, chopped

2 garlic cloves, crushed

1 teaspoon Szechuan chili powder

1 large red bell pepper, cored, seeded and
  cut into strips

1 large yellow bell pepper, cored, seeded and
  cut into strips

4 ounces firm tofu, cut into ½-inch cubes

¾ cups sugar snap peas or snow peas,
  topped and tailed

3 cups sprouted seeds

3 tablespoons chopped fresh sweet basil

¼ cup fresh ginger root, minced

1 tablespoon shoyu

fine sea salt and freshly ground black pepper

Not only is this a fast, highly nutritious feast, it looks good too. So what's the difference between noodles and pasta? Noodles usually have eggs in them while pasta doesn't necessarily. I am particularly fond of bean thread or cellophane noodles. These are made from bean gelatin and are vegan, and make a good filler for spring rolls. You can adapt the recipe to whatever you have in your store cupboard. Dry noodles or pasta will keep almost indefinitely in a cool dry place. Some Oriental noodles need soaking prior to use–30 minutes in cold water is more than adequate.

Sweet basil is a relative of ordinary basil but it is one fresh herb which complements Oriental cooking perfectly. It is often available from Chinese supermarkets–if you can't get sweet basil use ordinary basil or cilantro instead.

1 Cook the noodles according to the package instructions.

2 Meanwhile, heat the oil in a wok or large skillet. When the oil is very hot, add the scallions, garlic and chili powder. Stir-fry for 30 seconds before adding the peppers and tofu. Cook for 4 minutes.

3 When the noodles are ready to be drained and served, toss the sugar snaps or snow peas, sprouted seeds, sweet

basil and ginger into the wok and stir-fry for 1 further minute before adding the shoyu and seasoning. Stir in the noodles, mix well and serve immediately.

Serves 4

Fragrant Carrot and Cannellini Soup

3 tablespoons extra-virgin olive oil

1 large onion, chopped

2 garlic cloves, crushed

2 teaspoons cumin seeds

1 pound carrots, topped and tailed and sliced

1 large potato, chopped

4 cups hot vegetable stock

¾ cup dried cannellini beans, soaked overnight and cooked according to the package instructions (see note below)

fine sea salt and freshly ground black pepper

a little plain yogurt, sour cream, or shredded cheese, for serving (optional)

1 bunch of cilantro, chopped, for garnish

There's nothing better than a good soup in times of distress. When you are pregnant a good quick soup is an ideal meal. Soups can always be extended or added to, to make a more substantial meal.

1 Heat the olive oil in a large heavy-bottom saucepan. Add the onion and sauté gently for 2 minutes. Stir in the garlic and cumin seeds and allow the seeds to cook well. Add the carrots and potato and cook for a further 3 minutes. Pour in the vegetable stock and bring back to a boil, then reduce the heat to a simmer.

2 When all the vegetables are tender, purée them in a blender or food processor, or rub them through a strainer. Adjust the consistency of the soup by adding a little more stock or water if necessary, and season well with salt and freshly ground black pepper.

3 Return the soup to the rinsed saucepan, add the cooked cannellini beans and heat gently, stirring occasionally.

4 To serve, add a dollop of yogurt, sour cream or a little shredded cheese, if you like, and sprinkle with chopped cilantro. Serve immediately with your favorite croutons and organic whole wheat bread.

Serves 4

Note:
When cooking any dried beans that need soaking, boil them vigorously for 10 minutes prior to soaking overnight and skim off any impurities that rise to the surface. When finally cooked, these beans will be very easy to digest.

Spicy Lentils

1 tablespoon sunflower oil

2 garlic cloves, crushed

1 red onion, chopped

1 large carrot, shredded

1 teaspoon garam masala

1 teaspoon fennel seeds

1 teaspoon cumin seeds

1 teaspoon cilantro seeds, crushed

2¼ cups red lentils

1¾ cups canned chopped tomatoes

fine sea salt and freshly ground black pepper

1 bunch of cilantro or basil, chopped, for garnish

When Kate was pregnant with Mollie I would quite often find her cooking something like this. On asking her why, she would reply that she just felt like lentils–good old basic lentils. They are very quick to cook, full of protein and they are surprisingly delicious. This dish would make a good accompaniment to a more elaborate curry but stands on its own, too. If you're not in the mood for spice then simply omit it and rename the dish!

1 Heat the oil in a large heavy-bottom saucepan. Add the garlic, onion, carrot and spices and stir-fry for about 5 minutes. Add the red lentils and stir-fry for a further 3 minutes. Stir in the chopped tomatoes and enough water to cover the lentils and leave it to simmer for about 30 minutes. Alternatively, transfer the lentils to a baking dish and finish cooking them in the oven on a low heat.

2 Season to taste and serve the lentils topped with chopped cilantro or basil.

Serves 4

Variations:
If cooking in the oven, top the lentils with a little shredded cheese. If you like, sweeten the dish naturally by adding a few golden raisins or raisins.

A variation for a simple yet delicious alternative to Spicy Lentils. (See page 52.) Heat 1 tablespoon sunflower oil in a large heavy-bottom saucepan. Add the crushed garlic and the chopped red onion and stir-fry until the onion starts to blacken. Add the red lentils and cook for another 3 minutes, then add the canned chopped tomatoes and cook as before. This method of cooking red lentils produces a wonderful smoky flavor but may not appeal to everyone, especially children.

Tim's Spanish Omelet

1 tablespoon extra-virgin olive oil
1 red onion, finely sliced
1 garlic clove, crushed
1 red bell pepper, cored, seeded and diced
1 green bell pepper, cored, seeded and diced
1 cup cooked waxy potatoes
4 eggs (large size) from free-range chickens, beaten
fine sea salt and freshly ground black pepper

I don't know why, but I always feel a bit strange writing recipes that are so well known. But Spanish omelets are invariably cooked badly. We started cooking Spanish omelets at the restaurant when Tim (our head chef's boyfriend) suggested that it might be a good breakfast food. He is somewhat of a "Spanophile" and he makes a jolly good omelet. Quick to make, omelets are nutritious and attractive and just as good hot or cold. They're also excellent for using up leftovers, especially vegetable leftovers. What you need is a well-loved cast-iron skillet or tortilla pan, free from any residual baked-on food. If you are going to be cooking for just yourself and, of course, your "lump," then it is well worth investing in an individual omelet pan.

Spaniards like their omelets undercooked–although this is not recommended for pregnant women–and will often eat them like a sandwich between hunks of fresh, crusty bread.

1 Heat the oil in your skillet or omelet pan. Add the onion, garlic and peppers and cook for 3 minutes. Remove from the heat and tip the vegetables into a bowl. Add the eggs, mix in well, season then return the mixture to the skillet.

2 Cook over a moderate heat until set then gently ease the omelet away from the sides of the pan with a spatula and, with the help of a suitably sized plate, turn the omelet over so the other side can color. Cook for 1 further minute then serve.

Serves 4

Steamed Baby Vegetables with Lime and Walnut Dressing

2 cups baby potatoes, whole

2 cups baby carrots with green tops still attached

2 cups baby zucchini, zucchini flowers still attached

½ cup tender asparagus tips

2 cups baby corn

½ cup sugar snap peas

DRESSING:

1 shallot, finely chopped

1 tablespoon clear honey

3 tablespoons freshly squeezed lime juice

⅔ cup walnut oil

½ teaspoon mustard powder

fine sea salt and freshly ground black pepper

You will only be able to make this dish at certain times of the year, depending on the seasonal availability of some of the vegetables.

If you can't afford a proper steaming outfit, measure your large saucepans and find a cheap Chinese bamboo one that will fit as they cost very little.

This is a lovely dish to make just for yourself although you must be careful to undercook any vegetables that you are going to re-heat later in the day.

1 Bring a large saucepan of salted water to a boil. Add the whole potatoes and cook for 14 minutes or until tender.

2 Meanwhile, set up your Chinese bamboo steamer above the potatoes. They usually have at least two levels. After about 8 minutes put the whole baby carrots in the bottom level nearest the steam. After 3 minutes add the whole zucchini to the carrots and place the asparagus tips, whole baby corn and sugar snaps in the top layer. With any luck they should all be ready when the potatoes are cooked.

3 While the vegetables are steaming, make the dressing simply by mixing the dressing ingredients together very well.

4 Serve the vegetables with a good spoonful of vinaigrette on hot plates (simply cooked vegetables such as these will go cold very quickly otherwise).

Serve

Variation:

Try other vegetables like baby cauliflower, green beans, broad beans, baby turnips, and parsnips, baby leeks, baby eggplants, and even cherry tomatoes.

A BABY!

At last he or she has arrived and all that matters is that the baby is healthy, happy and, ideally nursing. I won't push the point, whole books have been written on the subject; but, to put it in a nutshell, infant preparations could be classed as cheap wine while breast milk is vintage champagne. Having said that, many mothers cannot nurse for a variety of reasons and so must take even more care when the time for introducing solids comes.

For the first 3-5 days of a baby's life, he or she will be sucking colostrum from their mother's breast. It is very high in vitamin A and new-born babies need it to develop healthy mucous linings in the eyes, nose, and lungs. A baby who receives this colostrum is less likely to develop bronchial infections, so even if long-term nursing is not an option it's worth battling away for the first week to make sure the baby has its fair share of vitamin A. It is widely recognised that most of our natural immune systems develop better in nursed babies than in bottle-fed babies. A breastfed baby will also be better equipped to move on to solids gradually when the time comes, simply because they will find they can eat a wider variety of things with little or no allergic reaction. One good reason for this is because breast milk will gradually be gently flavored by what the mother is eating and drinking. It may well be that mothers with gastronomical tastes develop gastronomically aware babies through their breast milk. Infant preparations just can't compete!

Times vary, but from 4-6 months there will come a stage when your baby is definitely looking for a little extra snack. If your supply of milk is copious you are unlikely to notice this so much but you may be noticing that feeding sessions are getting longer and longer. If your milk supply is not so prolific and you are already adding a feed of infant preparation, then it looks like the time has come to let some new taste buds loose on the world of food.

Initially you will give your baby a little extra at the end of a normal feed. As the demand for more increases there will come a point, and only you can judge it, when the extra comes first and the breast comes second. You've achieved the first step in weaning your baby. There are some very important things to remember when introducing your baby to solids.

1 Do not give your baby refined sugar in any shape or form—it is not worth even using honey (75% sugar) at this stage. The human body has no need of it; it is addictive, and is better for your baby's taste buds not to recognize it.

2 Do not give your newborn any extra salt. Too much salt in a baby's diet will damage his or her kidneys. Many pre-prepared baby foods contain more salt than is necessary.

3 Remember, your baby's body is still growing and developing. He or she may not be able to cope with some foods yet, especially if bottle-fed. Allergic reactions to basic foods can continue throughout childhood but particularly up to the age of five. To help identify any rogue foods it's worth, while still partially nursing, giving your baby purées of single foods, perhaps with your own milk, cow's milk or soya milk.

Six Months Plus

As I said at the beginning of the chapter, cooking is an act of love and caring. What is more important at this stage of your child's life than food prepared by his own mother or father? Prepared foods are great in emergencies or when travelling, but as a rule, cook for your baby yourself whenever possible. By cooking you will remain in touch with what is probably the most important time in a child's development. Babies have excellent natural palates and will appreciate a wide range of natural flavors after several months of nothing but milk, albeit flavored by mom. New tastes will be great adventures and one thing is for sure, if the customer in this case does not like his meal he will quickly and efficiently reject it! Babies thrive on fresh, lightly cooked vegetables, ripe raw fruits (not strawberries or citrus fruits early on) and easily digested protein such as egg yolk, tofu, curd cheese, yogurt, whole wheat cereals, beans and peas.

Avoid added fats as far as you can but do use whole milk and butter where needed rather than low-fat milk or chemically produced margarines. In fact, where necessary, use unrefined cold-pressed oils if you can. At six months though, these items don't really come into the equation. The following are some of the basic food stuffs with tips on how to use them.

1. Milks

a) Cow's milk should be introduced really carefully. If introduced too soon it will upset a baby's allergic system. It should never be given to babies under six months. Seven to eight months is an ideal time to use it, for softening purées of various foods and as a supplement to breast milk. Cow's milk should always be boiled before being given to a baby.

b) Soya milk is a good substitute for cow's milk and is suitable for use with a six-month-old baby. It may lack a few of the vitamins here and there but you can always make these up with fresh vegetables and fruit.

c) Goat's or ewe's milk is probably not worth using with vegetarian babies as both milks lack a lot of important vitamins. The best thing about these milks is their low sodium content.

2. Milk products

Yogurt is an excellent source of protein and calcium. The bacteria it contains also aids young babies' digestive systems, helping to avoid stomach upsets. Yogurt may be used on its own from six months onward or can be diluted with sterile water. It can also be added to fruit or vegetable purées, as can soft cheeses such as ricotta, and mascarpone. Avoid soft cheeses with rinds and goat's or ewe's cheeses.

Cheese is another milk product that your baby will enjoy. Use mild vegetarian Cheddar or curd cheese; try to avoid vacuum-packed soft cheeses. Cheese should never be overcooked as your baby will not be able to digest it. Use it combined with vegetables, grains, beans, or fruit.

3. Eggs, grains, beans, and bean products

These are essential building blocks for your baby. If you don't eat eggs I would recommend substituting tofu instead. It is almost as good nutritionally, although not quite so versatile, and much easier to digest.

Eggs, of course, must be well cooked and babies under eight months should not be given egg whites. Always buy fresh eggs from free-range chickens with a recent packaging date.

Cereals and grains should be added to your baby's diet with as much caution as milk and milk products. Rice is probably the best to start with. Ideally, use organic brown rice as it has a very low incidence of allergic reaction compared to wheat and wheat products. If you are able to, use ground rice initially as it takes much less time to cook and is easier for babies to digest. Cereals supply vital energy for your baby with important vitamins, nutrients, and trace elements, plus the all-important protection of dietary fiber. Don't go crazy, though. Very young digestive systems can only cope with a meal that is high in cereal fiber once a day. You can also use porridge oats–a wonderful traditional cereal, nourishing, palatable and superb for a quick, healthy breakfast. Properly prepared beans and peas are an excellent source of protein and other nutrients for babies of six months and older. All are easy to purée and combine well with other foods.

4. Fresh fruit and vegetables

These are all vital for life, with their vitamins, minerals and, of course, fiber. Avoid canned fruits and vegetables with the exception of some beans and peas, corn, tomatoes and unsweetened fruit, if desperate. Baked beans are best made at home where you can control the sugar content. Most fresh fruit needs little or no cooking. Vegetables, of course, vary, but if given the option always tend to undercook or leave raw succulent or leafy vegetables. Some root vegetables and tubers must be properly cooked, but not cooked to death. If you can, buy high-quality organic foods. Always buy good, firm, undamaged produce. Encourage your baby to eat fruit and vegetable skins as long as they have been well washed and cooked if necessary. Frozen fruits are excellent substitutes when fresh fruit is not in season and variety is essential to stimulate your baby's appetite. Dried fruits make marvelous healthy snacks as your baby gets older but because they are lower in vitamins and higher in sugar content than fresh fruit they are best used as a sweetener for young babies' desserts, should it be necessary. Fruit spreads with no added sugar are excellent for flavoring yogurts, soft cheeses and cereal puddings.

5. Seeds and nuts

Babies must not eat whole seeds or nuts but they can be ground or turned into spreads and then added to dishes. Peanut and other nut butters, tahini (sesame-seed paste) or corn oil paste are all ideal products.

6. Drinks

Apart from breast milk, try water (sterilized until the baby is six months old), diluted, freshly squeezed, and strained juices from fruits and vegetables and any unsweetened fruit juice (all our children developed an early addiction to unsweetened, diluted apple juice). Fruit juice can be diluted to 1 part juice to 8 parts water, gradually increasing the strength as your child gets older. All fruit juices should be used within 2-3 days once opened.

7. Pasta

Pasta is an ideal food product for small babies. To begin with, mash cooked, whole wheat, organic pasta with the rest of your ingredients. As your baby gets older, simply chop it up and the baby or toddler will be able to eat whole pasta. The smaller varieties, like gnocchetti or tubetti, are the most suitable.

A TYPICAL DAILY MENU
FOR A 6 TO 18-MONTH-OLD BABY

At this age the weaning process will probably have gently started. Most babies will be sleeping through the night so meal times will bear much more relation to adult meal times. The child's taste buds will have been awakened by the occasional purée offered before nursing in the preceding two months. Start to introduce tiny amounts of onion, garlic, and herbs into the meals.

It is most important to watch your baby at all times when he is feeding at this age, as it is very easy for babies to choke on small pieces of food. Equally, though, as the teeth develop so your baby should be given every opportunity to use them. This phase of your child's life really covers the transition from baby food to family food. By 18 months most children will be eating cut-up versions of the elder brother and sister's food. If he or she is your first child, then get into the habit of setting aside portions of your own food before you add loads of chili or Parmesan cheese!

Avocado, tofu, tahini, yogurt, red lentils, and pasta all make an ideal basis for quick meals if you are in a hurry and can often be extended into something for yourself.

It is also important to pay as much attention as possible to the color and texture of your baby's food, for as their senses develop so do their demands on you to provide not just tasty food but nice-looking food as well. All too often baby food is presented as a bland mass of gluey-looking mush.

TYPICAL MENU FOR A 6-18-MONTH-OLD BABY

ON WAKING FIRST THING: Very diluted apple juice, warm or cold (not chilled)

BREAKFAST: 8-9 AM
Winter: Porridge Oats with Fresh Apple and Yogurt
Summer: Baby Muesli with Fresh Peach Purée and Yogurt

to drink: Breast or diluted cow's milk, or diluted juice

LUNCH: 12-1:30 PM
Winter: Cauliflower and Pasta Cheese
                           Fruit and Vegetable Crudités
                           Plum and Tahini Custard Cream
Summer: Lentil and Vegetable Ragoût
                           Breadsticks
                           Raspberry and Tofu Cream

to drink: Diluted fruit or milk drink

DINNER: 3.30-5:30 PM
Winter: Butter Bean Winter Warmer
                           Cut-Up Avocado
                           Pear and Nut Crumble
Summer: Fresh Spinach Risotto
                           Baby Hummus
                           Fresh Nectarine Yogurt
to drink: Breast or diluted cow's milk

BEDTIME: 6-7 PM   Breast or diluted cow's milk

Porridge Oats with Fresh Apple and Yogurt

4 tablespoons cow's or soya milk
1 heaped tablespoon rolled oats
1 Macintosh, Ladyapple, or other small eating apple,
   peeled, cored and shredded
1 tablespoon plain yogurt

This is a very simple breakfast, but very nutritious and perfect for cold winter mornings. If you're worried about the size of the rolled oats, give them a good "whizz" in a blender or food processor.

1 Bring the milk to a boil in a stainless steel saucepan. Sprinkle on the oats, bring back to a boil, then simmer for 1 minute.
2 Stir in the shredded apple and cook for a further 3 minutes. If it is a little dry, add 3 tablespoons of water. Serve topped with a small dollop of yogurt.

Serves 1 very small person

Variations:
Replace the apple with other fruit such as pears or plums, or a fruit purée, a nut or seed butter or a little of both.

Fresh fruit purées for babies are made by mixing fruit with water or milk or both. Hard fruits should be lightly cooked or shredded; soft fruits can be pulped. In all cases, pits, seeds, and indigestible or blemished skins should be removed. If the fruit used is too acidic, sweeten it with a little date purée or natural fruit juice concentrate. Date purée is made by cooking natural dates in a little water, then straining or liquidizing them.

Dried fruits are excellent for making "instant" purées. In most cases soak the fruit overnight, then poach for 30 minutes, or until tender. Save the water from cooking to soften the purée or to offer as a drink. When the fruit is cooked, drain before liquidizing or straining. Good dried fruits for puréeing are apples, apricots, dates, figs, prunes, raisins, and golden raisins.

Baby Muesli with Fresh Peach Purée and Yogurt

1 teaspoon wheatgerm
1 tablespoon rolled oats
1 tablespoon sunflower seeds
1 teaspoon seedless raisins
1 tablespoon cashew nuts
5 tablespoons milk or water
1 ripe peach, peeled, halved and pitted
1 tablespoon plain yogurt

Baby muesli is best made at home. Avoid using wheat products initially, then, as your baby grows, introduce them gradually. For small babies, you must "whizz" the dry ingredients in a blender or food processor prior to use.

1 Combine the dry ingredients, cover with the milk or water and soak for 10 minutes, or bring to a boil in a small saucepan and simmer for 5 minutes. Older babies can eat the muesli uncooked with either hot or cold milk.
2 Mash the peach, then mix with a fork. Combine the peach and muesli and serve topped with plain yogurt. If it's a little dry, serve with extra milk.

Serves 1 very small person

Variations:
Vary the dry ingredients: try ground rice, corn meal, or millet (all should be cooked), or add nut or seed pastes like peanut butter or tahini. Substitute dates or figs for raisins.

Try other additions such as any fruit purée, shredded fresh hard fruit, soya milk, quark or even a homemade fruity yogurt.

Overleaf Left—CAULIFLOWER AND PASTA CHEESE, PLUM AND TAHINI CUSTARD CREAM *Right*—CRUDITES

Cauliflower and Pasta Cheese

1 cup cauliflower, broken into small flowerets
⅓ cup organic whole wheat pasta (the smallest size available)
3 tablespoons cow's or soya milk
1 heaped teaspoon baby rice
1 tablespoon vegetarian mild Cheddar cheese, shredded
1 teaspoon wheatgerm

There is little necessity to use ready-made meals from jars or packages and you will feel much happier knowing your baby is eating good fresh food full of natural goodness such as this. (It is suitable for younger babies if liquidized.)

1 Poach the cauliflower in a little boiling water in a saucepan for 8 minutes. Save the water and cook the pasta in it according to the package instructions.

2 Meanwhile, bring the milk to a boil in another saucepan, add the baby rice, stir, and simmer until it thickens. Remove from the heat and add the cheese, cauliflower and pasta.

3 Depending on your baby it may be necessary to mash the mixture a little. Otherwise, sprinkle it with wheatgerm and put under a preheated broiler for 1 minute to color slightly.

Serves 1 very small person

Variations:
Vegans could replace the cheese with tofu.

Try using other vegetables such as broccoli, leeks, zucchini, mushrooms (for older babies only), spinach, and fresh peas. The pasta can be replaced with almost any grain, bean, or pea your baby likes.

Try adding small amounts of garlic, nutmeg, or herbs. The dish could also be enriched by a hard-boiled egg yolk.

Crudités

COOKED CRUDITÉS:

cauliflower flowerets
broccoli flowerets
kohlrabi, cut into sticks
artichoke hearts, halved
asparagus spears, cut into small sections lengthwise
fennel, lightly poached and dissected
celery, cut into small lengths
zucchini, as above
parsnips, as above
carrots, as above
celeriac, as above
potato, as above

RAW CRUDITÉS:

gem lettuce
Chinese leaf ribs
tomatoes, peeled, seeded, and chopped
peppers, peeled, cored, seeded, and cut into strips
avocados, pitted and sliced
mushrooms, whole
apples, peeled, cored, and sliced
apricots, pitted
banana, sliced
cherries, pitted
grapes, seeded and halved
mango, pitted and cut into strips
melon, sliced
peach, pitted
pear, peeled, cored, and sliced

Sticks of vegetables are great for your baby's first attempts at self-sufficiency. As early as six months some babies will show an inclination to feed themselves. Because they have few teeth, if any, they must be supervised since they are inclined to choke. Initially, vegetable strips may be cooked to aid the eating process. As soon as you can, reduce or eliminate the cooking.

You'll soon learn which vegetables and fruits your baby prefers—keep experimenting and eliminate the unpopular ones.

Note that waxed skins on fruit and vegetables can be de-waxed only by soaking in hot water. If this is too much trouble, remove the skin.

For 1 very small person

Plum and Tahini Custard Cream

3 large ripe plums, peeled, halved and pitted

1 teaspoon date syrup or date purée (see page 61)

1 egg yolk (large size). Vegans can use 1 teaspoon soya
    flour plus 2 teaspoons cornstarch

¾ cup whole milk or soya milk, brought to
    a boil

1 teaspoon tahini

tiny pinch of freshly ground nutmeg

It is well worth making fruit purées when fruit are in season (see page 61). They are inexpensive, filling, nutritious and a real treat for the whole family when nothing interesting is available. Babies are particularly appreciative of new flavors and textures.

1 Mash the plums with a fork and add the date syrup or purée.

2 Beat the egg or flours, if using, boiling milk, tahini and nutmeg together in a small saucepan. Combine all the ingredients well and bring back to a gentle boil. Simmer for 3 minutes.

3 Pour into 4 ramekins, cover with foil and stand in an ovenproof dish containing enough hot water to cover half the depth of the ramekins. Cook in a preheated oven, 325°F, until set, about 25 minutes. Serve chilled.

Serves 4

Lentil and Vegetable Ragoût

3 tablespoons brown lentils

2 canned or fresh tomatoes, peeled, seeded
    and chopped

1 teaspoon minced onion (only for older babies)

1 tablespoon tomato juice, or juice from the
    canned tomatoes

4 tablespoons water

½ cup carrots, finely diced

¼ cup zucchini, finely diced

1 tablespoon corn

1 basil leaf, torn into pieces

1 tablespoon vegetarian mild Cheddar cheese, shredded
    (optional)

1 tablespoon organic whole wheat bread crumbs,
    finely ground

This is a real treat for those tiny taste buds and it looks good too.

1 Soak and precook the lentils: boil quickly in a large pan of water for 10 minutes; remove from the heat, soak for 12 hours, then cook until tender for about 40 minutes.

2 In another pan, bring the tomatoes, onion, if using, tomato juice and water to a boil. Add the carrots, cook for 10 minutes, then stir in the zucchini, corn, lentils, and basil, and simmer for another 10 minutes—all the vegetables should now be tender.

3 For very young babies, liquidize or mash the mixture. Pour into a greased baking dish and top with the cheese, if using, and the bread crumbs. Place under a preheated broiler until golden.

Serves 1 very small person

Variations:

Use other dried beans, cereals or peas—haricot and kidney beans are especially good, but make sure they are well cooked.

Try fresh vegetables such as green beans, mushrooms (for older babies only), cauliflower, or broccoli.

Try enhancing the sauce with nut or seed butters and pastes such as peanut butter or tahini, or enrich the sauce with a little milk, cream cheese, or yogurt.

Breadsticks (Grissini)

1 teaspoon active dried yeast
1¾ cups unbleached white bread flour, plus
  1 tablespoon
1 cup warm water
1 teaspoon unsalted butter, at room temperature
2 teaspoons extra-virgin olive oil, plus extra
  for oiling
fine sea salt

Bread sticks are perfect for babies to munch, once you have established they are not allergic to wheat. What is more, these breadsticks are sugar-free, which is more than can be said for store-bought ones.

1 In a small clean bowl mix the yeast with the 1 tablespoon of flour and add 4 tablespoons of the water. Cover and set aside in a warm place to start frothing.

2 In a large clean bowl mix together the remaining flour with a good pinch of salt, then form a well in the center of the flour. Add the yeast mixture, then the remaining water, gradually working it well into the flour by hand or with a wooden spoon. When all the liquid has been absorbed knead the dough quickly, turning the bowl at the same time. It will take about 4 minutes and you will know that you have achieved the right consistency when the dough stops sticking to the sides of the bowl.

3 Place the dough on a floured surface and knead it again for up to 20 minutes. Yes, it is a long time, and exhausting!

4 Return the dough to the cleaned bowl and form a well in the center. Add half of the butter and 1 teaspoon of the oil and gradually work in. Initially the dough will fall apart; keep it up–it will come good in the end.

5 Lift the dough out of the bowl. Use the remaining oil to grease the bowl and replace the dough. Turn the dough in the bowl so that it is coated in a thin layer of olive oil. Place a damp dish cloth over the bowl and leave in a warm place for about 1 hour, or until doubled in bulk.

6 Turn the dough out on to a lightly floured surface and knock back a few times before spreading it out with your fingers to form a rectangle, about 4 x 6 inches. Fold about ½ inch of the longest edge toward you and then tightly roll the whole thing up to form a Swiss roll. Tuck the final edge into the bottom of the roll to make a neat seam. Brush with oil, cover and set aside to rise again for 1 hour or, again, until doubled in bulk.

7 Oil a baking sheet. Cut the roll crossways into twelve ¼-inch lengths.

8 Hold the ends of each piece of dough and gradually pull, stretching each piece into a breadstick about 12 inches long. Lay each stick on the baking sheet about 1 inch apart. Spray generously with water and place immediately in the hottest part of a preheated oven, 425°F. Bake for 6 minutes, then spray again and bake for a further 20 minutes or until golden brown and crisp all the way through. Remove from the oven and allow to cool on a wire rack.

9 Breadsticks will keep in an airtight jar in a dark cool place for several weeks.

Makes 12

Raspberry and Tofu Cream

1 heaped tablespoon fresh or frozen raspberries, thawed
½ teaspoon organic apple juice concentrate
2 ounces soft tofu
1 tablespoon plain yogurt or sour cream
a little whole milk

Tofu is an excellent, nutritious, and easily digestible food for babies. Try this with a delicious fresh fruit purée (see page 61).
1 Push the raspberries through a strainer to remove any seeds. Add the rest of the ingredients and mash or blend in a blender or food processor to the desired consistency.
Serves 1 very small person

Variations:
Use any soft fruit, uncooked, or any hard fruit which has been gently poached. Sweeten with date purée (see page 61) or a little honey or even fructose.

Try adding a little curd cheese or baby rice, or add banana as a sweetener or simply as a filler.

Cut-Up Avocado

½ a firm avocado

Avocados are a perfect meal for young babies. (All of our children have enjoyed them.) Six to eight-month-old babies can easily eat half a ripe avocado.
1 Halve the avocado, leaving the stone intact in one half.
2 Remove the skin from the pitted half and cut into finger food or simply serve directly from the skin with a teaspoon.
Serves 1 very small person

Variations:
Very ripe avocados may be puréed with a little lemon or lime juice. Alternatively, combine an avocado with cheese, yogurt, nut or seed pastes, or even fruit purées, cooked where necessary.

Butter Bean Winter Warmer

½ cup water
½ cup carrots, finely diced
½ cup parsnips, finely diced
2 teaspoons finely chopped onion (only for babies over 8 months)
¼ cup celery, finely diced
2 button mushrooms
4 tablespoons well-cooked butter beans
pinch of dried thyme

It can get chilly sitting in a stroller in mid-winter while parents are shopping, so here's a dish to provide some natural heat.
1 Bring the water to a boil in a saucepan, add the carrots and parsnips, and simmer for 10 minutes. Add the rest of the ingredients and simmer until tender. Serve the dish as is, or purée, or part-purée the vegetables before serving.
Serves 1 very small person (over 8 months old)

Variation:
This dish can be enriched with milk, cream cheese or yogurt.

Pear and Nut Crumble

corn oil, for oiling

1 small, ripe pear, peeled, cored
   and sliced

a few drops of lemon juice

½ teaspoon organic apple juice concentrate

1 tablespoon ground almonds

1 tablespoon organic whole wheat flour

pinch of ground cinnamon

1 teaspoon unsalted butter or cold-pressed oil

This dish can be enjoyed by the whole family.

1 Lightly oil a ¼-inch ramekin with corn oil. Layer the pear in the bottom of the ramekin. Sprinkle with the lemon juice and apple juice concentrate and enough hot water to half cover the fruit.

2 Place the ground almonds, flour, cinnamon, and butter in a bowl. Rub together with your fingertips until the mixture resembles fine bread crumbs. Sprinkle over the pear and bake in a preheated oven, 350°F, for 45 minutes.

Serves 1 small person

Variations:
Substitute the pear with apples, peaches, apricots, and almost any properly poached fruit. Add dried fruit such as chopped dates or golden raisins to naturally sweeten, and add regular oats or oatmeal to the crumble mix.

Fresh Spinach Risotto

5 tablespoons boiling water

1 tablespoon Basmati or other long-grain white
   rice, washed, and well drained

1 fresh tomato, peeled, seeded, and chopped

1 teaspoon finely chopped onion (optional)

¼ cup fresh spinach, roughly chopped and large
   stalks removed

1 tablespoon shredded vegetarian mild Cheddar
   cheese, or crumbled tofu

2 teaspoons cream cheese or yogurt

This exotic-sounding combination of rice, fresh vegetables, and dairy produce is an almost perfect balance of nutrients and vitamins for your baby.

The dish is best eaten fresh but can be re-heated in the oven or microwave. Younger children will enjoy it liquidized or partially liquidized.

1 Place the boiling water, rice, tomato, and onion, if using, in a small saucepan and bring to a boil, then simmer for about 10 minutes.

2 Add the spinach and continue to simmer for another 4 minutes or until the rice is tender–all of the water should have been absorbed. Stir in the cheese and cream cheese or yogurt and serve immediately.

Serves 1 very small person

Baby Hummus

¼ cup cooked chick-peas (see below)

3 teaspoons tahini

½ teaspoon lemon juice

2 teaspoons extra-virgin olive oil

3½ tablespoons chick-pea water or ordinary boiled water

¼ teaspoon chopped garlic (optional)

It is best to make this when you are making hummus for the rest of the family. It freezes well so you can freeze several portions for the baby at the same time.

To prepare the chick-peas, soak them overnight, drain, then cook in fresh water for about 1½ hours or until very tender; drain.

1 Place the cooked chick-peas with the rest of the ingredients in a blender or food processor and blend to a smooth paste.

2 Serve accompanied by freshly cut cucumber sticks if your baby is old enough, otherwise serve the hummus on its own.

Serves 1 very small person

Fresh Nectarine Yogurt

1 ripe nectarine, peeled, halved, and pitted

3 tablespoons yogurt

Strawberries may be out for tiny babies but fresh ripe nectarines are definitely in. Use only ripe, undamaged fruits.

1 Mash the fruit with a fork or purée it in a blender or food processor. Stir into the yogurt and serve.

Serves 1 tiny person

Field Mushroom Fondue

2 tablespoons butter

2 shallots, finely chopped

2 cups field mushrooms, roughly chopped

1 cup white grape juice or apple juice

3 teaspoons cornstarch

4 cups vegetarian mild Cheddar cheese, shredded (adults may enjoy Gruyère, Emmenthal, or Jarlsberg)

½ teaspoon dried English mustard

fine sea salt and freshly ground black pepper

½ loaf of soft unbleached white or organic whole wheat bread, cut into cubes

Rather an exotic dish for a baby you might say. This dish will happily feed two adults and several children, so for small families halve the quantities. It will probably be more appreciated by older babies who can get their gums around chunks of bread dipped into the cheese and mushroom mixture. For adults only, substitute white grape juice with white wine and add lots of garlic and some chopped basil leaves at the end.

1 Melt the butter in a heavy-bottom saucepan, add the shallots, and cook until softening. Stir in the mushrooms and cook for 3 more minutes. Blend a little grape juice with the cornstarch.

2 Add the rest of the grape juice to the mushrooms, bring to a boil and reduce by half. Stir in the cornstarch and when the mixture has thickened add cheese, mustard, and salt and pepper to taste.

3 Dip in chunks of bread and set a few aside to cool.

Serves 4

SCHOOL DAYS

They say that school days are the "happiest days of your life," although it is generally said retrospectively. Nevertheless, it is true, but can really only be put into perspective in hindsight. Little do we know when we leave school that things are going to get worse!

With two or more children at school, the days simply rocket past so that there is scarcely time to breathe let alone cook, talk, relax, or even plan. But plan you must, especially meals, otherwise life will turn into an unending treadmill where food is at best boring and at worst positively bad for you and your children. Remember that once children go to school their appetites immediately double and you are no longer in charge of their taste buds. This is potentially a very serious state of affairs. I do believe that a lot of petty crime, vandalism, and hooliganism stems from the poor diet of a lot of young people today. In many cases it is because both parents have to work, but in lots of cases it is simply down to lack of planning, motivation, and know-how on the part of the parents. Cooking for your family, it seems, is no longer considered a priority and in some families it seems impossible. Problems often arise because the male in the family can't or won't cook. More than ever before, all the family members should be made aware of the differences between healthy food and garbage and family participation in the preparation of meals is essential.

SCHOOL DAY BREAKFASTS

Breakfast is the most important meal of the day, but when everyone is rushing off to school and work it can be a nightmare, with many families settling on cereal or toast as their "kickstart" to the day. There's nothing wrong with cereal or toast as they can be highly nutritious. Cereals should be as natural as possible with no added sugar. Bran flakes or wheat flakes are excellent examples and, like whole meal toast, should be organic. Toast should be spread with a little unsalted butter and topped with sugar-free jam or suitable savory spreads. If you like milk with your cereal make sure that your children have whole milk even if you prefer low-fat milk yourself. I was spoiled by my mother who, despite having three children, found time to cook each of us exactly what we wanted every morning, which sometimes meant cooking eggs in three different ways! The breakfast recipes in this chapter are chosen for speed, taste and nutritious content—the sort of meals you can prepare and put on the table in a maximum of 20 minutes.

Egg-Stra Bread

8 slices of your favorite loaf, 1½ inches thick, cut diagonally and with "pocket" formed (see below)

1 cup cream cheese

½ cup peanut butter, at room temperature

4 ripe bananas, sliced

8 eggs, beaten

1½ cups milk

½ teaspoon vanilla extract (optional)

3 tablespoons sesame seeds

1 stick butter

This is quick and easy to prepare, very nourishing, and fun, too. There's no need to buy special ingredients—unless you want to! Egg-stra bread can be wholesomely savory or stunningly sweet depending on your mood and your family's preference. The concept is simple: Take a thick slice of your favorite bread (day-old bread is best) and cut it in half diagonally. With a knife, cut a pocket into the bread along the length of the diagonal, being careful not to cut through the crust. This is filled with your favorite filling, soaked in a mixture of egg and milk, and then fried. Egg-stra Bread can be prepared the night before and left soaking in the egg mixture overnight, if you're very short of time.

1 Spoon the cream cheese and peanut butter into the bread "pockets." Slip the bananas in with your fingers, making sure the pockets are evenly filled.

2 In a bowl beat the eggs, milk, and vanilla extract. Add the bread "pockets" and let them soak for 2½ minutes on each side, then dip in sesame seeds to coat all over.

3 Heat 2 tablespoons (¼ stick) of the butter in a skillet and fry the bread on both sides until golden brown. Keep the "pockets" warm in the oven while you fry the rest, using the rest of the butter as necessary. Serve, dusted with a little frosting sugar or fructose, if you like.

Serves 4

Variations:

With cream cheese try jam, puréed compote and fruit.

With shredded Cheddar cheese try cooked mushrooms, raw tomatoes and fresh herbs, roasted bell peppers, or pickles and chutneys.

With peanut butter, try tahini, miso, or tofu.

Fruitfast

2 ripe honeydew or galia melons, halved and seeded

1½ cups fresh raspberries

juice of 1 orange

1 cup plain yogurt or sour cream

1 tablespoon wheatgerm

1 tablespoon clear honey

A fruitfast, not surprisingly, centers breakfast around fresh vitamin-packed fruit. From a health point of view, probably the best thing to enter your stomach after the forced fast of sleep is fruit. Not only does it wake you up, it also wakes up your digestive system in a natural and gentle way, giving you energy and vitamins. Fruitfast takes the nutritional side one step further with its inclusion of wheatgerm and yogurt—both good for us.

Fruitfasts should be made literally just before eating.

1 Place the melon halves on 4 plates. Fill them with the fresh raspberries and douse them in the freshly squeezed orange juice. Top with the plain yogurt or sour cream, sprinkle with wheatgerm and trickle over some honey.

Serves 4

Scrambled Skins

2 large baking potatoes, scrubbed

a little vegetable oil or melted butter

4 eggs (or 6 if not using cream) from free-range chickens

¼ cup heavy or light cream, or milk

shredded vegetarian Cheddar or mozzarella cheese
   (optional)

chopped fresh chives or basil (optional)

Sometimes a slight change in the way you present food can make all the difference as to whether your children will eat it or not. For some reason, and despite the fact that baked potatoes are healthy and nutritious, most children actually enjoy them. Filled with creamy scrambled eggs they make a quick and easy breakfast that will definitely become a favorite.

1 The night before, prick the potatoes, place in a preheated oven, 400°F, and bake until they are tender, about 1-1¼ hours. When cooked, hollow them out, leaving a reasonably substantial shell. (Keep the potato to use later, perhaps for making hash browns to serve with the Scrambled Skins.) Wrap each potato shell in foil and refrigerate.

2 In the morning brush the skins inside and out with a little vegetable oil or melted butter. Place them in a preheated oven, 400°F, and let them cook to golden and crispy, about 20 minutes.

3 Meanwhile, slowly cook the scrambled eggs, they'll take about 20-30 minutes using the following technique. Try this recipe at least once; it belies the myth that scrambled eggs should be beaten, and actually cooks them without butter or oil.

4 Break the eggs into a cast-iron saucepan. Add the cream or milk and stir the two gently until well blended. Introduce heat to the pan slowly and gently, stirring only occasionally. Avoid letting the mixture boil and season only just before serving. Add the cheese and herbs, if you're using.

5 Pile the eggs into the potato skins and serve immediately.

Variations:

Scrambled eggs can be the medium to convey many good things into your children's stomachs. Just stir almost anything you like into the egg mixture in the latter part of the cooking procedure. Some ingredients will have to be precooked and some are fine added just as they are. The variations are endless; here are some suggestions:

Almost any dairy produce you enjoy, such as heavy cream, cream cheese, plain yogurt, blue cheeses, or hard cheeses can be added.

Try adding vegetables such as spinach, onions, tomatoes, bell peppers and eggplants, mushrooms, or asparagus tips.

Apple and Raisin Porridge

1 cup barley flakes

1 cup jumbo oats

2 cups regular oats

⅓ cup raisins

3¾ cups apple juice

2 apples, peeled, cored, and chopped

1¾ cups milk

½ teaspoon ground cinnamon

Porridge can be made from any flaked grain, meal, or flour and you can use a mixture of cereals. All of these cereals are best if soaked in their future cooking liquid overnight—not only does this make the cereal more digestible, but it also speeds up the cooking time.

1 Soak the barley flakes, all of the oats, and the raisins in the apple juice overnight.

2 Place in a large saucepan, add the apples, the milk, and the cinnamon and bring to a boil. Simmer, stirring frequently, for 15-20 minutes or until the oats are cooked.

3 Serve the porridge with more milk or yogurt or cream and a little honey to sweeten, if you like.

Serves 4

Big Breakfast Bran Bars

a little oil, for oiling

⅔ cup organic regular oats

1¼ cups organic whole wheat flour

¾ cup apple juice

¼ cup wheatgerm

¼ cup oat bran

¾ cup raisins

½ teaspoon ground cinnamon

⅓ cup soft brown sugar

1 tablespoon molasses (optional)

½ cup sesame seeds

1 cup chopped mixed nuts

⅓ cup soya oil

This is emergency breakfast material when the children have suddenly discovered homework they had to do or piano they had to practice or perhaps you just got up late. Despite being made of breakfast-type foods, they are good at any time of the day and should be made at least weekly and stored in a sealed box or bag in the refrigerator.

1 Grease a 10 x 12-inch baking pan and line with wax paper.

2 Combine all of the ingredients in a large bowl and mix thoroughly with a wooden spoon. Pour into the prepared pan, making sure the mixture reaches right into the corners. Avoid pressing the mixture down to prevent making a solid "concrete" breakfast bar.

3 Bake in a preheated oven, 350°F, for about 45 minutes, until golden brown. Cut into squares or rectangles while still hot but don't attempt to remove from the pan until they are totally cool.

Serves 4

Peach Blintzes with Loganberry Sauce

CREPE BATTER:

3 eggs from free-range chickens, beaten

1 cup organic whole wheat flour

1 cup water or milk, or both

½ teaspoon clear honey or maple syrup

about 1 tablespoon butter, for cooking

LOGANBERRY SAUCE:

1½ cups fresh loganberries

1 teaspoon clear honey

1 drop vanilla extract

1 teaspoon arrowroot

¼ cup water

PEACH FILLING:

3 sweet, juicy peaches, peeled,
   pitted and sliced

3 tablespoons unsalted butter

juice of ½ a lemon

1 tablespoon clear honey

2 tablespoons golden raisins

¼ teaspoon ground nutmeg

Apart from wondering, "What on earth are blintzes?" I bet you're thinking, "He's crazy." Blintzes are filled crêpes and, yes, I am suggesting that you have them for breakfast. In actual fact, crêpes can take less time to make than omelets, especially if you make the crêpe mix the night before. Crêpe batter improves with age—up to 24 hours—because the particles of flour start to break down in the egg/milk/water mix making it a smoother batter.

So we've now established that making crêpes that are simply served with lemon and honey or maple syrup are easy, you will find that filling them does not take much more effort. It's just a question of quickly sautéing some succulent fruit or vegetables in butter and perhaps a little lemon or orange juice. Blintzes can be
sweet or savory and sweet blintzes can also have a sauce, which is quick to make. I would suggest definitely making the sauce the day before or freezing several sauces from time to time when fresh fruits are in season. And when it's all done, watch the children wolf them down. Here's a delicious recipe for fruity blintzes that will make a summer's day shine for sure.

1 Make the batter by blending the eggs, flour, water or milk, and honey or syrup together in a bowl to form a smooth creamy liquid. This must be done at least 30 minutes before the crêpes are cooked. If you have made the batter the night before, give it a quick whisk in the morning before using, as it will have "settled out" overnight. The batter must be refrigerated when it is not being used.

2 For the loganberry sauce, heat the loganberries gently in a saucepan with the honey and vanilla. Blend the arrowroot with the water and when the loganberries are boiling fold it in. Alternatively, simply pass the loganberries through a strainer to make a delicious coulis. This sauce can be frozen or kept in the refrigerator overnight.

3 To make the filling, stir-fry the peach slices in the gently bubbling butter for 3 minutes. Add the rest of the ingredients and remove from the heat.

4 Melt a little butter in a 8- or 9-inch skillet or crêpe pan. Add about 4 tablespoons of the batter to the pan and cook the crêpe for about 1 minute on each side. Continue in this way until all the batter has been used up, keeping the crêpes warm in the oven until ready to use.

5 When ready to serve, place a little peach filling on each crêpe, roll up carefully, and serve immediately, topped with the warmed loganberry sauce.

Serves 4

Variations:

Try different combinations of fillings and sauces: banana and chocolate, apple and blackberry, or strawberry and rhubarb. Try a savory filling like cheese and mushrooms, or baked beans.

Nutty Banana Muffins

¼ cup coarse unsalted, sugar-free cashew
   nut butter

2 large bananas, mashed

1 cup plain yogurt

4 tablespoons clear honey

2 eggs from free-range chickens

1¼ cups organic whole wheat flour, sifted

¼ cup soya flour, sifted

1 teaspoon ground cinnamon

1 teaspoon baking powder

1 teaspoon baking soda

¼ cup sunflower seeds, toasted

a tablespoon butter or vegetable oil, for greasing

¼ cup unsweetened jam

¼ cup cashew nut pieces, for decoration

Muffins are a great way to start the day; they are quick, easy to make, and versatile. Hot muffins straight from the oven are good on their own or with jam and butter.

Muffins can be baked earlier, frozen, and re-heated wrapped in foil when required. You can freeze the uncooked mixture in the muffin pans or paper cases and when you want to cook them, add 10 minutes on to the cooking time. Alternatively, keep the batter in the refrigerator and use some as you need it. The batter will keep for up to 5 days but the rise you get will diminish with age. The most important thing with any muffin is quality of ingredients, so get muffin making.

1 Mix the cashew nut butter, the bananas, yogurt, honey, and eggs together in a bowl. In another bowl combine the flours, cinnamon, baking powder, and baking soda. Combine the wet and the dry ingredients, then stir in the sunflower seeds.

2 Grease 12 muffin pans. Pour enough mixture into each pan to half fill, add a teaspoon of jam then fill to the top with more muffin mixture.

3 Sprinkle the muffins with cashew pieces, then bake them in a preheated oven, 400°F, for about 25 minutes or until golden brown.

Serves 12 (or 36 tiny ones)

Pear and Plum Compote

1¼ cups dried pears, soaked overnight in warm
   water with a little vanilla extract, and ½ cup of
   the soaking water reserved

¾ pound plums, pitted

½ cup maple syrup

½ stick of cinnamon

a little shredded lemon peel

3 tablespoons lemon juice

juice of 1 orange

Compotes can always be made in advance ready to be eaten at any time. Make a large batch and keep in the refrigerator. If you've made it right it won't be there long! Compotes are wonderful healthy foods that are good on their own or on top of, for example, cereal. I like them best served with a good dollop of plain yogurt or sour cream.

1 Place all the ingredients together in a large pan. Heat gently, stirring occasionally, until the fruits are soft, about 20-25 minutes. Allow to cool, then cover and refrigerate.

2 Serve the compote cold with a heavy and creamy accompaniment such as cream, sour cream or plain yogurt.

Serves 4

LUNCH BOX TREATS, SNACKS, AND SUPER SUPPERS

For children who don't eat school lunches, a brown bag lunch is vitally important, although, having made sure that they have good breakfasts and dinners, snack lunches can be sufficient. There is virtually no control over what is brought to school in a lunch box and all too often "one-up-manship" leads to a child having to have a store-bought chocolate bar included so as to be the same as his or her friend. There is no need for schools to stretch limited budgets by buying meat and meat substitutes like TVP (textured vegetable protein), when with more care and attention they could feed children more healthily and effectively with fresh vegetables, fruits, dairy produce and the vast selection of grains, beans, peas, seeds, nuts, and pastas available today. If the meal looks and tastes good then children – certainly most children – will eat it. Indeed, increasingly at schools where there is a vegetarian option children are choosing this option because it looks and smells more exciting.

Quite simply your child's brown bag lunch has to be good. Take, for example, the standard lunch box of sandwich, bag of chips, chocolate bar, piece of fruit, and drink. We will look at each of these items in a little more detail and suggest some healthy alternatives.

When school is over and the children are home the first thing they want is something to eat. It can't be too big or it would spoil their appetite for supper; it's likely to be small, tasty, and probably sweet – homemade cookies or cakes are ideal, or some fruit, cut up if necessary. And then to supper, your child's main evening meal. Children's friends may be involved at short notice so meals must be flexible, easy to bulk out and occasionally a treat. Day-to-day family suppers generally center around pasta, pastry, potatoes, and bread. Make the dishes elaborate or simple, depending on money, mood, and time.

SANDWICHES

First and foremost, sandwiches need good bread. Other considerations must be how to fill it, does it need to travel, and should it be served hot? Here are a few ideas that you can use for a lunch box treat, a snack or a dinner-time treat. All of these recipes are suitable for five year olds and upward.

To return to bread, there is no point in buying whole wheat bread unless it is made with organic flour. The pesticides used to spray wheat stay only in the husk, so if it's not organic bread buy unbleached white bread. Unless you're toasting it, the bread must be as fresh as can be. In France bakers make bread twice a day, often three times a day, because the French people have never accepted that bread should be more than four hours old at the time of eating. Sandwiches in lunch boxes need to be less messy than those eaten at home, first because they have to travel, and second because it avoids your child coming home with, for example, great splashes of mayonnaise all over their clothes. Here are some really delicious but not too messy fillings for sandwiches.

Herby Cream Cheese Spread

¼ cup cream cheese
6 tablespoons (¾ stick) butter, melted
2 garlic cloves, crushed, or ½ bunch of scallions, chopped (optional)
1 tablespoon snipped fresh chives
½ tablespoon chopped fresh parsley
½ tablespoon chopped fresh chervil
fine sea salt and freshly ground black pepper

This filling is ideal with cucumbers, tomatoes, onions, and almost any vegetable or leaf you would use in a salad. Try it with nuts or bananas, too.

1 Place the cream cheese in a bowl. Beat the cooled melted butter into it quickly. Add the rest of the ingredients and season. Set aside in the refrigerator until required.

Makes 1 pound

Note:
To soften the spread add a little milk, yogurt or cream.

Avocado and Tomato Dip

2 large ripe avocados
2 scallions, finely chopped
1 large tomato, peeled and chopped
juice of 1 lime
a little chopped cilantro, to taste (optional)
1 garlic clove (optional)
¼ teaspoon chili powder (optional)
fine sea salt and freshly ground black pepper

This has to be made fresh as avocados oxidize quickly, but goes well with salad vegetables, particularly sprouted seeds. You could even combine it with refried beans in a soft flour tortilla (see page 128) to really set the pace at lunchtime. Failing tortillas, use pita bread or taco shells.

1 Mash the avocados in a bowl and mix in the remaining ingredients, combining well – do not blend or purée the mixture. Use immediately.

Enough for 4 sandwiches

Mushroom "Spread"

½ cup (1 stick) butter

4 shallots, finely chopped

2 pounds field mushrooms, finely chopped

3 cups butter beans, cooked

3 tablespoons lemon juice

fine sea salt and freshly ground black pepper

Another versatile and natural "spread" to have around if your children like mushrooms. It's good in sandwiches (hot or cold), choux pastry, tarts, and pies.

1 Melt the butter in a pan. Add the shallots and cook until beginning to soften. Add the mushrooms, cover, and cook very gently until very soft, as long as you can, preferably about 1½ hours. If there is a lot of liquid, remove the lid after 1 hour and let it evaporate.

2 When cool, place the mushrooms in a blender or food processor. Add the butter beans and lemon juice and purée to a spread-like consistency. Season to taste.

Makes lots

Hummus

1 cup chick-peas

1 tablespoon tahini

1 teaspoon ground cumin

3 cloves garlic, crushed

juice of 1 lemon

⅓ cup extra-virgin olive oil

pinch of paprika (optional)

fine sea salt and freshly ground black pepper

Hummus is another firm favorite with children. It will keep well in the refrigerator for up to two weeks, or you can freeze it. It is full of goodness and goes well with all the vegetables you would use in salads.

1 Soak the chick-peas overnight.

2 Drain the chick-peas, then cook in fresh water for 1½ hours or until very tender. Drain reserving some of the cooking liquid.

3 Put the remaining ingredients in a blender or food processor and blend together. Add the chick-peas and mix well. If the mixture is too stiff, add a little of the chick-pea water until the mixture is the right consistency.

Makes lots

Crunchy Egg Spread

4 eggs from free-range chickens, hard-boiled
  (see below)

1 small bell pepper, cored, seeded, and finely diced

1 celery stalk, finely chopped

3 scallions, finely chopped

4 pickles, finely chopped (optional)

1 garlic clove, crushed

1 teaspoon capers, finely chopped

1 teaspoon mustard powder

1 cup mayonnaise

fine sea salt and freshly ground black pepper

To hard boil an egg while retaining its flavor and nutritional value is a simple but under-practiced art. Carefully place a large egg in a pan and cover with cold water. Bring to a boil, turn off the heat, and let the egg sit in the hot water for 6 minutes, then tip out the water and replace with cold water. Smaller eggs require less time. Peel the egg but only cut into it when ready to use or eat.

1 Place all of the ingredients in a bowl and mash together. Adjust the seasoning to taste. Use in sandwiches, together with mustard and cress, if you like.

Enough for 4 sandwiches

ALTERNATIVES TO SANDWICHES

Sandwiches don't have to mean just two slices of ordinary bread with something in between. There is a vast array of alternatives, all of which demand their own exciting fillings. Choose from croissants, biscuits, speciality breads such as focaccia, pita bread, naan bread, and tortillas. Here are just a few ideas; all of which are equally good combined with the basic spreads on pages 81-82.

Cress and Cream Cheese Croissant

2 fresh croissants
½ cup cream cheese or herby cream
  cheese spread
½ cup of sprouted mustard seeds and cress

A decent croissant needs no extra butter. Try filling croissants and serving them cold for a lunch box or serve hot at home.
1 Split the croissants in two and spread cream cheese thickly on each bottom half, pile on the sprouted mustard seeds and cress and replace the top half of the croissant. Wrap in foil for transporting in a lunch box.
Makes 2

Alternative fillings:
If your child likes Brie, try a little with redcurrant jelly and a few lettuce leaves.

Use pâtés such as Walnut and Cream Cheese Pâté (see page 20) with lettuce and tomatoes, or fill croissants with mozzarella cheese, tomato, and a herby mayonnaise.

Savory Cheese Biscuits

⅓ cup cream cheese
2 cups unbleached all-purpose white flour
1½ teaspoons baking powder
½ teaspoon salt
1 garlic clove, crushed
2 teaspoons finely chopped fresh mixed herbs
1 teaspoon dried mixed herbs
½ cup milk
beaten egg or milk, for glazing
½ cup shredded cheese, for topping

Biscuits are often overlooked as alternative sandwich casings. These biscuits can be frozen uncooked, then popped in the oven as and when you want them. Serve split in half and buttered, or filled with a pâté or Mushroom Spread (see page 82), topped with a dollop of mango chutney and lettuce and tomato garnish.
1 In a large bowl rub the cream cheese into the flour, baking powder, salt, garlic, and herbs with your fingertips until the mixture resembles fine bread crumbs.
2 Quickly stir in the milk to form a soft dough and shape it into a ball with floured hands.
3 On a lightly floured surface gently roll out the dough to a

Overleaf Left- HUMMUS, PAIN BAGNAT, CRESS AND CREAM CROISSANT *Right —* CRUDITES, AVOCADO AND TOMATO DIP, SAVORY CHEESE BISCUITS, PAIN BAGNAT.

thickness of 1 inch and cut out the biscuits using a 2-inch round cookie cutter.

4 Brush the tops with egg or milk to glaze and sprinkle with shredded cheese. Place on a lightly greased baking sheet and bake in a preheated oven, 425°F, for 10-15 minutes or until they are well risen and golden brown.

5 Remove from the oven and serve immediately if you're eating them at home; otherwise allow to cool before filling.

Makes 6

Pain Bagnat (Bathed Bread)

1 large ripe tomato, cut into chunks

½ cucumber, peeled and cut into similar size chunks

1 red bell pepper, cored, seeded and cubed (broiled first, if you like)

4 scallions, chopped

4 leaves of bok choy, chopped

1 cup bean sprouts or sprouted seeds

1 tablespoon cashew nuts, roasted

8 black olives, pitted (optional)

4 artichoke hearts, sliced (optional)

1 cup vegetarian Cheddar, mozzarella, feta, goat's cheese or tofu

4 crusty organic whole wheat or unbleached white rolls, the tops removed and centers hollowed out

TOMATO AND BASIL VINAIGRETTE:

3 teaspoons Dijon mustard

1 tablespoon tomato paste

½ cup basil leaves, torn into pieces

4 tablespoons white wine vinegar

1 dessertspoon soft brown sugar

2 garlic cloves, crushed (optional)

1 cup extra-virgin olive oil

fine sea salt and freshly ground black pepper

Originating in southern France, this is my sort of food: a crusty bread roll which becomes a "container" for salad. The hard bread "shell" soaks up any excess dressing. Try spooning some of the Mushroom Spread (see page 82), Walnut and Cream Cheese Pâté (see page 20) or hummus into the roll before adding salad and dressing.

1 For the vinaigrette dressing, whisk all the ingredients except the oil together in a jug. Gradually add the oil, whisking all the time. Season to taste.

2 Mix all the salad ingredients and then spoon them into the hollowed-out rolls. Cover with the vinaigrette and then replace the lids. Serve immediately.

Makes 4

Variations:

Try adding favorite marinated vegetables such as mushrooms, eggplants and zucchini or pickled onions, pickles and cauliflower. Avocado and cooked beet root are delicious, too.

Try other salad leaves such as chicory, gem lettuce, or rocket.

HOT SANDWICHES

The following recipes are no good for brown bag lunches but make great snacks at home. All you need is a broiler and an excellent imagination. Keep planning to a bare minimum – use up what's in your refrigerator and cupboards.

Croque Enfant

8 large slices of unbleached white bread

1 tablespoon French mustard

1 cup brown mushrooms, sautéed in butter

1 bunch of chives, snipped

1 cup Edam, Emmenthal or Gruyère cheese, freshly shredded

½ cup (1 stick) softened butter

In France the only hot sandwiches are Croque Monsieur (bland béchamel and slimy ham) and Croque Madame (bland béchamel with a frankfurter). No great sandwich has developed in France because, on the whole, they do not recognize the need for a quick snack – a meal is a meal and lasts for at least two hours. So here is my alternative – Croque Enfant – a broiled open sandwich that most children will love as a snack or for dinner.

1 Put the slices of bread on a work surface, spread with some mustard and top with the sautéed mushrooms. Sprinkle with the chives. Cover the mushrooms evenly with the shredded cheese. Put the remaining slices of bread on top.

2 Butter the outside of the sandwiches and place on a baking sheet. Bake in a preheated oven, 425°F, for about 5 minutes or until crispy and golden on both sides. Alternatively, cook in a sandwich toaster.

Makes 4

Variations:

Substitute broiled or sautéed vegetables such as bell peppers, tomatoes, eggplants or onions for the mushrooms. For a vegan sandwich, replace the cheese with broiled marinated tofu.

Gruyère and Tomato Toasts

2 garlic cloves, crushed (optional)

3 tablespoons extra-virgin olive oil

1 French bread, cut diagonally into 12 x ½-inch thick slices

4 vine-ripened fresh plump tomatoes, each cut into 3 slices

1½ cups Gruyère or vegetarian Cheddar cheese, shredded, or sliced into 12 portions

fine sea salt and freshly ground black pepper

basil leaves, torn into small pieces, for garnish

1 Mix the garlic, if using with the olive oil, and brush one side of each bread slice with it. Toast both sides of the bread under the broiler until lightly browned. If necessary, brush a little more oil on the sides of the bread. Top each with tomato, season, then top with cheese and season again.

2 Place on an oiled baking sheet and cook in a preheated oven, 375°F, or under the broiler for 6-8 minutes until the cheese is bubbling. Sprinkle with basil and serve.

Makes 12

Variations:

Use mozzarella or goat's cheese. Substitute bell peppers, eggplants, onions or mushrooms for the tomatoes.

Overleaf Left – GRUYÈRE AND TOMATO TOASTS, HEY PRESTO PIZZA, CHEESY CORN AND MUSHROOM MUFFINS *Right* – GRUYÈRE AND TOMATO TOASTS, CHEESY CORN AND MUSHROOM MUFFINS

Cheesy Corn and Mushroom Muffins

2 tablespoons butter, plus extra for greasing

1 small leek, white part only, finely chopped

1 cup open cup mushrooms

¾ cup organic whole wheat flour

½ cup milk or water

½ cup vegetarian Cheddar cheese, shredded

1 cup frozen or drained, canned corn

2 eggs from free-range chickens, beaten

¼ cup wheatgerm

¼ cup cornmeal

1 teaspoon dried oregano

2 teaspoons baking powder

1 teaspoon baking soda

fine sea salt and freshly ground black pepper

TO GARNISH:

a little shredded cheese

sesame seeds

1 Melt the butter in a pan and cook the leeks for about 3 minutes, add the mushrooms and cook for 5 minutes. Stir in 3 tablespoons of the flour and cook for about 1 minute.

2 Gradually add the milk to make a sauce, stir in the cheese and the corn. Set aside.

3 In a bowl combine the eggs, wheatgerm, cornmeal, the remaining flour, oregano, baking powder, and baking soda. Season lightly.

4 Grease 12 muffin tins with a little butter.

5 Combine the vegetable mixture with the flour mixture and spoon into the muffin tins. Sprinkle the muffins with a little cheese and sesame seeds and bake in a preheated oven, 400°F, for 20 minutes. Serve as a snack or with steamed vegetables as a meal.

Makes 12

Welsh Crumpets

1½ tablespoons butter

3 tablespoons organic whole wheat flour

1 cup dark beer

2¼ cups vegetarian Cheddar cheese, shredded

1 large tablespoon prepared English mustard

1 garlic clove, crushed (optional)

4 English muffins

fine sea salt and freshly ground black pepper

This is a variation of Welsh Rarebit – crumpets are in fact of Welsh origin, too. Serve 2 crumpets per child and 4 for adults. They are ideal for a child's dinner.

1 Make the sauce by melting the butter in a small pan and whisking in the flour until well combined. Gradually add the beer, whisking continuously to make a thick sauce. Stir in the shredded cheese and mustard, season to taste and add the crushed garlic, if using.

2 Cut the muffins in half and place them upside down under a preheated broiler and toast until lightly browned. Remove from the broiler, turn over, and top with a spoonful of the cheese sauce. Put them back under the broiler until they are golden brown.

Makes 8

Variation:

Top the crumpets with tomato, cooked onion or mushrooms before adding the cheese sauce.

Hey Presto Pizza

6-inch focaccia (plain olive oil or onion flavor is
  excellent)
1 tablespoon olive oil
2 garlic cloves, crushed
1 large onion, finely sliced
1 red bell pepper, cored, seeded and finely sliced
1 tablespoon tomato paste
6 tomatoes, sliced
1 cup mozzarella or vegetarian Cheddar cheese, or a
  mixture of the two, shredded
3 teaspoons dried basil
fine sea salt and freshly ground black pepper

*Just about every child in the world likes pizza, and since they are
so easy to make at home I don't understand why people buy
them. Okay, you buy them to save time, but they don't take any
time anyway. If you want a ready-made base see if your supermarket stocks focaccia before buying the vacuum-packed bases.
This Italian flat bread is one of the origins of pizza and the moist
dough, rich with olive oil, re-heats beautifully. Just top an individual small focaccia or a large one with your favorite topping
and away you go.*

1 Place the focaccia on a well-oiled baking sheet.

2 Heat the olive oil in a small heavy-bottom skillet. Add the
garlic and cook for a few minutes. Add the onion and pepper and
cook for another 2 minutes.

3 Spread a little tomato paste on to each focaccia. Top with the
tomato slices and pile the cooked onions, garlic, and peppers on
to the top.

4 Mix the shredded cheese with the basil and seasoning and
sprinkle over the pizzas. Place in a preheated oven, 425°F, and
bake for 15-20 minutes until golden brown. Serve with a salad of
crisp- leaved lettuce.

Makes 4

"Sausage" Rolls

2 tablespoons vegetable oil
1 onion, finely chopped
1 celery stalk, finely chopped
2 teaspoons dried thyme
1 cup flat mushrooms, finely chopped
¾ cup red lentils
1 cup water
1 tablespoon tomato paste
3 tablespoons peanut butter
1 tablespoon shoyu
1 garlic clove, crushed (optional)
¾ cup whole wheat bread crumbs
2 packages puff pastry, thawed if frozen
fine sea salt and freshly ground black pepper
beaten egg, for glazing
1 tablespoon sesame seeds, for decoration

Our sausage rolls are without meat and will appeal to everyone.

1 Heat the oil in a pan, cook the onion, celery and thyme until
beginning to soften. Add the mushrooms and lentils and cook for
2 minutes. Stir in the water, tomato paste, peanut butter, shoyu,
and garlic. Cover and cook gently for 20 minutes.

2 Fold in the bread crumbs and season, set aside to cool. If the
mixture is very chunky purée half of it in a blender or food processor then return to the remaining mixture and mix together.

3 On a lightly floured surface, roll out the pastry to a 6 x 24-inch
rectangle. Spoon the filling down the center of the rectangle,
moisten one long edge of the pastry and fold over. Seal by crimp-
ing or by hand.

5 Brush with beaten egg yolk and sprinkle with sesame seeds.
Cut across into 20 small or 10 big rolls. Refrigerate for 30 minutes
prior to cooking. Bake in a preheated oven, 425°F, for 25 minutes
until well risen and golden brown.

Makes 36

Empanadas

1 tablespoon extra-virgin olive oil

½ teaspoon chili powder

½ teaspoon ground cumin

1 onion, finely chopped

1 garlic clove, crushed

1 cup chestnut mushrooms, sliced

1 red bell pepper, cored, seeded, and finely cubed

8 ounce can corn, drained

2 large ripe tomatoes, peeled and chopped

½ tablespoon tomato paste

½ cup vegetarian Cheddar cheese, shredded

½ cup mozzarella cheese, shredded

¾ quantity of tortilla dough (see Mexican Fajitas
    and Frijoles, page 128)

olive oil, for frying

fine sea salt and freshly ground black pepper

*Empanadas are a Spanish version of English pasties,
Russian piroshkis, Turkish boreks and Indian samosas.
Empanadas were originally made using bread dough. Here
I've suggested using floury tortilla dough (see page 128) but
if this is inconvenient use frozen puff pastry. Empanadas
may be deep fried, baked, or shallow fried. They are good
hot or cold and make a great supper or lunch box filler.*

1 To make the filling, heat the oil in a skillet, stir in the
spices, onion and garlic, and sauté until beginning to soften.
Add the mushrooms and peppers and cook for 5 minutes.

2 Stir in the corn and tomatoes and cook for another 5 minutes before adding the tomato paste and seasoning. Set
aside to cool before folding in the cheeses.

3 To assemble, the dough must be rolled out very thinly so
it is best to prepare it in small pieces. Cut the pastry into
circles with a 3¼-inch diameter round cutter.

4 Spoon a little filling into the center of each circle, dampen
the edges, fold over and crimp together to seal.

5 Fry the empanadas in about ½ an inch of hot oil in a skillet until golden. Drain on paper towels and serve with a
good salsa, salad, and boiled potatoes. Alternatively, serve
cold on their own or with relish.

Serves 4

Spinach and Potato Hash

⅓ cup extra-virgin olive oil

2 onions, cut into wedges

1 pound potatoes, very thinly sliced

2 garlic cloves, crushed (optional)

2 teaspoons chopped fresh chives, thyme,
    or parsley

½ cup fresh spinach, stalks removed

4 eggs from free-range chickens, beaten

½ cup mozzarella or vegetarian Cheddar
    cheese, shredded

fine sea salt and freshly ground black pepper

*Here is a dish to get vital vitamins down eager young
throats. It's quite simple and versatile, and best made with
leftover vegetables.*

1 Heat the oil in a casserole dish. Add onions and potatoes,
seasoning, garlic and herbs, and sauté for 5 minutes until
well coated in oil and the potatoes start to color. Place the
casserole dish in a preheated oven, 400°F, for 25 minutes.

2 Remove the dish from the oven and stir in the spinach and
eggs. Sprinkle cheese over the top and return to the oven.
Bake for 10 minutes or until the eggs are set, then serve.

Serves 4

Variation:
*Use shallots instead of onions and replace the spinach
with broccoli, bell peppers, eggplant, or tomatoes.*

ESSENTIALLY SWEET

Of course no brown-bag lunch or special supper would be complete without a little something sweet. Anything from good, ripe, whole fresh fruit to homemade chocolate chip cookies falls into this category. These tasty recipes are simple to make and range from delicious Apple Sauce Cake, tempting Golden Raisin and Peanut Butter Cookies to mouth-watering Banana Yogurt Cake and Very Fruity Bars.

These treats are particularly robust and are ideal for surviving the rigors of a lunch box, or filling that appetite gap children have when they come home from school. They keep well in an airtight container and are easy to make in bulk; in most cases they can also be frozen as back-up stocks for emergencies.

All too often we are consumed by guilt on biting into something evenly remotely sweet. Most of these recipes use a minimum of natural refined sugars and a maximum of fruit, to reduce that guilty feeling after a wonderful but sinfully rich treat. All children and adults will love them!

Apple Sauce Cake

CAKE:

½ cup (1 stick) unsalted butter

½ cup soft brown sugar

2 eggs (large) from free-range chickens, beaten

1 teaspoon vanilla extract

½ teaspoon shredded orange rind

2 cups organic whole wheat flour

3 teaspoons baking powder

½ teaspoon salt

1 teaspoon ground cinnamon

½ teaspoon ground allspice

½ cup nuts, chopped

⅓ cup raisins

1 cup unsweetened apple sauce

TOPPING:

4 tablespoons chopped mixed nuts

1 tablespoon butter

½ cup organic whole wheat flour

3 tablespoons soft brown sugar

½ teaspoon ground cinnamon

This is an extremely appetizing and nutritious cake that keeps well.

1 Cream the butter and the sugar together in a large bowl. Add the eggs gradually, then stir in the vanilla extract and orange rind.

2 In another bowl, combine the remaining ingredients – except the apple sauce – and fold carefully into the creamed mixture, then stir in the apple sauce.

3 Pour into a greased 8-inch round cake pan, leveling the surface. Mix the topping ingredients together and sprinkle over the top. Bake in a preheated oven, 325°F, for 1½ hours, or until a toothpick comes out clean.

4 Remove from the oven and allow the cake to cool in the pan before turning out.

Makes an 8-inch cake

Power Punch

2 cups Power Base (see below)

2½ cups fresh unsweetened orange, apple, or pineapple juice

2 ripe bananas, peeled and chopped

2 large apples, cored and roughly chopped

⅛ cup plain yogurt

Quite often there simply isn't much cake around or cookies in the cookie jar and you don't have time to make anything. "But I'm starving!" cry the children.

Power Punches consist of seeds, cereals, fruits, and dairy products (if you like) combined in a blender to make a smooth, satisfying, and energy-packed liquid refreshment. Don't feel confined to the suggestions in this recipe; just use your own ingredients. To simplify the procedure first decide on a base, then add to it when the occasion demands. Mainly cereal "power bases" like the one listed below can be kept in the refrigerator or freezer and used from frozen.

1 Simply blend all the ingredients together in a blender or food processor until smooth and serve with or without ice.

Serves 4

Power Base:

To make a Power Base, blend all of the following ingredients together until very fine, then store in the refrigerator or freezer. Use ¼ cup of Power Base per person.

¼ cup cocoa or carob powder

¼ cup wheatgerm

¼ cup coarse oatmeal

¼ cup sunflower seeds

¼ cup sesame seeds

1 package brewer's yeast, powdered

¼ cup powdered whole milk (optional)

¼ cup unsweetened shredded coconut

Ultimate Shortcake

1 cup organic whole wheat flour

½ cup ground almonds

½ cup (1 stick) butter

4 tablespoons soft brown sugar

½ egg yolk

pinch of salt

fine, unsweetened, shredded coconut, for dusting

Organic whole wheat shortcake can be delicious but once again it is the ingredients that count. This is a perfect family snack and far more satisfying than a packet of store-bought cookies. With judicious use of fresh fruits and cream you can turn it into a sumptuous dessert.

1 Mix the flour and the almonds together in a bowl. Add the butter and the sugar and rub in together. Stir in the egg yolk and salt. Mix well and knead to form a smooth dough.

2 Place an 8-inch flan pan on a lightly greased baking sheet and press the dough into it. Alternatively, roll the dough out to an 8-inch round if you don't have a flan ring – it will still taste as good. Lightly mark the shortcake into 8 wedges and then chill for about 30 minutes.

3 Place in a preheated oven, 325°F, and bake for 30 minutes or until pale golden brown. Remove from the oven, re-score the wedges, and dust with fine shredded coconut. Allow the shortcake to cool for 5 minutes only on the baking sheet, then lift off carefully using two spatulas and complete cooling on a wire rack.

Makes 8

Overleaf Left – BANANA YOGURT CAKE *Right* – APPLE SAUCE CAKE, GOLDEN RAISIN AND PEANUT BUTTER COOKIES, VERY FRUITY BARS

Very Fruity Bars

¾ cup pitted prunes

1 cup whole dried apricots

1 cup whole dried bananas, chopped into
 ½-inch pieces

1 cup raisins

1½ cups chopped mixed nuts

2 cups unsweetened shredded coconut

1 cup organic whole wheat flour

1 cup regular oats

⅓ cup soya oil

⅓ cup maple syrup or organic apple concentrate

1 teaspoon almond extract

1 teaspoon vanilla extract

¼ cup sunflower seeds

1 Place the prunes, apricots, bananas, and raisins in a large bowl. Pour in enough cold water to cover and leave them to soak overnight.

2 Grease a 10 x 12-inch baking sheet and line with greased wax paper.

3 Mix all of the ingredients together in a bowl. If the mixture seems too dry add a little more liquid from the soaked fruit. Tip the mixture onto the prepared baking sheet, gently pressing it into the corners and levelling the surface.

4 Bake for 30 minutes in a preheated oven, 325°F, or until golden brown. Remove and allow to cool before cutting.

5 Cut the bars into 3 lengthwise and into 6 across to make 18 rectangles that will fit nicely into a lunch box or airtight container. These bars keep very well, especially since they contain no dairy products.

Makes 18

Golden Raisin and Peanut Butter Cookies

2 eggs from free-range chickens

½ cup milk

¼ cup (½ stick) unsalted butter

½ teaspoon ground nutmeg

½ teaspoon ground cinnamon

½ teaspoon ground cloves

1 teaspoon vanilla extract

¾ cup chunky peanut butter

1 cup organic whole wheat flour

½ cup soya flour

1 teaspoon baking powder

½ teaspoon salt

¼ cup wheatgerm

⅓ cup golden raisins

These cookies are miniature feasts and combine all the nutrients growing children need as well as being great for adults, too.

1 Place the eggs, milk, butter, spices, vanilla extract, and peanut butter in a mixing bowl or food processor and mix together well.

2 In a separate bowl combine all the dry ingredients except the golden raisins. Combine the two mixtures together, fold in the golden raisins.

3 Line a greased baking sheet with greased wax paper and place spoonfuls of the cookie mixture on to the paper, spacing well apart and gently flattening each mound with the back of the spoon. Bake in a preheated oven, 450°F, for 8-12 minutes until golden brown.

4 Remove from the oven and allow to cool on a wire rack.

Makes 24

Date and Walnut Crunch Cake

BASE:

½ cup organic whole wheat flour

¼ cup soya flour

¼ cup wheatbran

¼ cup wheatgerm

2 tablespoons soya oil

1 tablespoon unsalted butter or vegan margarine

½ teaspoon vanilla extract

TOPPING:

¾ cup dried dates, soaked in ½ cup warm water overnight

1 tablespoon clear honey (optional)

1 cup walnuts, chopped

Make this cake another excellent yet robust addition to your ever-expanding repertoire.

1 For the base, mix all the ingredients together in a bowl or blend in a food processor until they resemble coarse bread crumbs.

2 Grease a 6 x 10-inch baking sheet and line with greased wax paper. Press three-quarters of the shortbread base mixture onto the sheet and bake in a preheated oven, 350°F, for 15 minutes.

3 Meanwhile, cook the dates briefly in the water in which they have been soaking. Stir in the honey, if using, and the chopped nuts. Spread evenly over the precooked base then top with the remaining shortbread mixture.

4 Return to the oven and cook for another 10 minutes. Allow to cool before cutting into 24 pieces.

Makes 24

Variation:

Substitute figs, prunes, or apricots for the dates and adjust the sweetening accordingly.

Banana Yogurt Cake

½ cup yogurt

¾ cup soft brown sugar

½ cup (1 stick) butter, melted, or

   ½ cup vegetable oil

2 very ripe bananas, mashed

2 eggs (large) from free-range chickens, beaten

1½ cups organic whole wheat flour, sifted

1½ teaspoons baking powder

pinch of salt

finely shredded rind of 1 lemon

This is a beautifully moist cake that positively explodes with goodness. It is good as is, or it can be dressed up to look quite fancy for a special occasion.

1 Grease an 8-inch cake pan with oil or butter and line with wax paper.

2 Beat the yogurt and sugar together in a bowl until smooth. Whisk in the melted butter or vegetable oil quickly, followed by the bananas and the eggs.

3 In another bowl sift together the flour, baking powder, and salt. Then carefully fold into the egg mixture and stir in the lemon rind.

4 Tip the mixture into the prepared cake pan. Place in a preheated oven, 350°F, and bake for 45-55 minutes or until firm to the touch. Turn out onto a wire rack to cool.

Makes an 8-inch cake

Variations:

This cake is good decorated with fresh summer fruits or unsweetened jam.

Alternatively, top with a wholesome cream cheese and lemon frosting, made by combining ½ cup cream cheese with the shredded rind, juice of ½ a lemon or lime, and ¼ cup light brown sugar. Top with a few strips of lemon or lime rind to decorate.

EVERYDAY DINNERS

These are the core of family life: work or school day dinners that are the very thread of existence. In most families they must by necessity be quick and easy to prepare and economically viable. If your children are prone to inviting friends back unexpectedly the meals must also be easily extendable. Ideally, they should be enjoyed by children and adults alike; adults often tend to eat later than children so everyday dinners should be good re-heated or else be to easy to set aside portions from for cooking an hour or two later. Everyday dinners have no set rules; everything that is cooked has to fit into your time scale. Therefore, it is quite probable that dessert will only appear after the simplest of main dishes and equally more complex dinner dishes will leave time only for fresh fruit or yogurt.

Picture the situation: "Mom, can Charlotte come to our house for dinner?" Having only just got back from work yourself, you hastily tossed together enough macaroni and cheese for you and your family, then dashed to school to pick up the children. Solution: buy cauliflower or some mushrooms on your way home. Poach the cauliflower or sauté the mushrooms before adding them to your macaroni and cheese. Alternatively, make a quick and healthy salad to accompany the macaroni. Nine times out of ten, an extra mouth to feed at a meal will be no problem unless the meal comes in portions like Bambeano Burgers or stuffed crêpes. For these times try to cook in batches and keep a few spare in the freezer. You'll find them an invaluable stock for unexpected occasions and guests.

EVERYDAY MAIN COURSES

Pasta, rice, potatoes, and bread are probably the fastest "instant" foods in our kitchen and consequently form the base of many everyday dinners. There's no reason why a perfectly good meal using the simplest of ingredients cannot be made within 20 minutes using such basic, nourishing, and solid foundations.

This chapter includes a few main meal pasta sauces that could equally top rice or potatoes. When using dried pasta, remember to allow ½ cup per person. Boil it in plenty of water, adding salt and oil only if you want to. When the pasta is cooked, season it, and serve immediately with butter or a drizzle with good fruity olive oil. If you are cooking the pasta in advance, immerse it quickly in cold water and leave under a cold running tap until cold, to stop the pasta sticking together.

Instant Fresh Tomato and Basil Sauce

3 tablespoons extra-virgin olive oil

1 large onion, finely sliced

3 garlic cloves, crushed

1 pound ripe tomatoes, peeled, seeded and chopped, the juice retained

20 basil leaves, torn into pieces

a little brown sugar or balsamic vinegar, to taste

fine sea salt and freshly ground black pepper

In almost the time it takes to open and cook a packet of instant tomato sauce this fresh sauce can be made using nature's very own instant ingredients—tomatoes, garlic, and basil. Make the sauce while the pasta is cooking.

1 Heat the oil in a skillet. Add the onions and garlic and cook until beginning to soften. Add the tomatoes and cook for a further 10 minutes. Stir in the basil, season, and add sugar or balsamic vinegar to adjust the acidity. Serve with pasta or rice topped with shredded Cheddar or Parmesan.

Serves 4

Variations:
Add bell peppers, mushrooms, corn, lentils, green beans, olives, and even a dollop of sour cream. Try other herbs like marjoram, parsley, or chervil.

Instant "Canned" Tomato and Basil Sauce

3 tablespoons extra-virgin olive oil

1 large onion, finely sliced

3 garlic cloves, crushed

1 dessertspoon soft brown sugar

1 tablespoon balsamic vinegar, or 3 tablespoons red wine vinegar

1 tablespoon tomato paste

2 x 12 ounce cans chopped tomatoes

20 basil leaves, torn into pieces

fine sea salt and freshly ground black pepper

Fresh tomatoes are often not what they should be. Picked green and forced to travel, many are barely suitable to use salads, let alone sauces. Here is a recipe using the finest canned Italian plum tomatoes. The trouble with canned tomatoes is of course the metallic flavor. This is easily removed with plenty of cooking but if you want to do it quickly other ingredients must be used, primarily vinegar and honey or sugar.

1 Heat the oil in a large heavy-bottom saucepan. Add the onion and garlic and sauté until beginning to soften and darken in color. Add the sugar and vinegar and reduce by half. Stir in the tomato paste, cook for 1 minute, then add the canned chopped tomatoes.

2 Bring to a boil and partially cover the saucepan to reduce the sauce and prevent your stove from being splattered with tomato juice. After 5 minutes stir in the basil and adjust the seasoning.

3 Allow the tomato sauce to simmer while cooking your pasta or rice.

Serves 4

Indonesian Peanut Sauce

1 tablespoon vegetable oil

1 large onion, finely sliced

½ teaspoon chili powder

1 teaspoon ground cumin

1 large green bell pepper, cored, seeded, and cut into small strips

2 garlic cloves, crushed

1 tablespoon soft brown sugar

¼ to ⅓ cup lemon juice

1 cup chunky peanut butter

1½ cups hot water

1 tablespoon shoyu

freshly ground black pepper

This is a really simple peanut sauce that can be adjusted to suit your children's taste buds. Serve it with Chinese egg noodles, pasta, rice, or as a topping for baked potatoes.

1 Heat the oil in large heavy-bottom saucepan. Add the onion, spices, and a little black pepper and cook gently for 5 minutes. Stir in the green pepper and garlic and cook for a further 5 minutes over a slightly higher heat.

2 Add the sugar and lemon juice, cook for 1 minute, stirring well. Fold in the peanut butter and quickly add the water, stirring to a smooth consistency. Bring to a boil, add the shoyu, and adjust the seasoning to taste.

3 Serve the sauce with rice or pasta with raw or steamed vegetables such as cucumber, yellow peppers, Chinese leaf, snow peas, bean sprouts, and chopped scallions; roasted whole peanuts are good here too. Sprinkle with a little finely shredded coconut or shredded cheese, if you like.

Cheesy Spinach and Mushroom Sauce

1 tablespoon butter

2 tablespoons unbleached all-purpose white flour

1 cup whole milk

1 cup vegetarian Cheddar cheese, shredded

½ teaspoon ground nutmeg

2 teaspoons mustard powder

4 ounces cherry tomatoes, halved and broiled

1 cup mushrooms, thinly sliced

1 cup fresh spinach, stalks removed

fine sea salt and freshly ground black pepper

Another very quick multi-functional sauce.

1 Melt the butter in a small saucepan and stir in the flour quickly to make a roux. Cook for about 1½ minutes. Set aside to cool for 1 minute and bring the milk to a boil in another saucepan.

2 Return the roux to the stove and gradually add the hot milk over a medium-to-high heat, stirring all the time. As the sauce thickens, more liquid can be added without curdling. Add the remaining ingredients, stir, and cook for 3 minutes over a low heat until all the spinach has wilted.

3 Adjust the seasoning to taste and serve on a bed of pasta, rice, or baked potatoes, topped with shredded Cheddar or Parmesan.

Serves 4

Variations:

Crumble in a little blue cheese and add a glass of white wine to the sauce.

Try adding lightly sautéed zucchini, broccoli, leeks, red or green bell peppers, and cauliflower.

Mexican Rice

4 tablespoons extra-virgin olive oil

1 large onion, finely chopped

1 red bell pepper, cored, seeded and cut into
   ½-inch cubes

1 green bell pepper, cored, seeded and cut into
   ½-inch cubes

1 cup button mushrooms, sliced

2 cups long-grain brown rice

1 pound ripe tomatoes, peeled, seeded, and chopped, or
   12 ounce can chopped tomatoes

3 garlic cloves, crushed

½ poblano or ancho chili

2 cups hot vegetable stock or water

1 cup dry white wine or vegetable stock

¾ cup fresh or frozen peas

¾ cup frozen, or drained, canned corn

¾ cup drained, canned kidney beans (the liquid can be
   used in the stock)

fine sea salt and freshly ground black pepper

3 tablespoons chopped fresh cilantro, for garnish

This rice dish is fresh, nutritious and colorful, including many favorite ingredients. The quantity of chili given in this recipe will make the dish only slightly spicy, so adjust it according to your family's taste. Poblano is a fresh chili, ancho is the dried version with the seeds removed.

Mexican Rice is a complete meal in itself or will make a good side dish for a Mexican dinner party.

1 Heat the olive oil in your largest, heaviest casserole dish. Add the onion and sauté for 5 minutes. Add the peppers and mushrooms and cook for a further 5 minutes before stirring in the rice.

2 Meanwhile, purée together the tomatoes, garlic and chili in a blender or food processor.

3 When the rice is well coated in oil, stir in the tomato paste and cook for 3 minutes.

4 Bring the stock or water and the wine to a boil and add it gradually to the rice mixture until all of the liquid has been absorbed and the rice is tender; this will take 15-20 minutes. Alternatively, add all of the liquid at once to the rice, stir once, then cover and leave for 15 minutes. Cook over a low heat to avoid burning.

5 Stir in the peas, corn, and kidney beans, cover and let finish cooking for 5 minutes. Season to taste and serve the rice garnished with freshly chopped cilantro.

Serves 4-6

Leek and Zucchini Stir-Fry

3 tablespoons extra-virgin olive oil

3 leeks, thinly sliced

2 zucchini, thinly sliced

1 large red bell pepper, cored, seeded, and
   thinly sliced

6 cups cooked pasta or rice

10 basil leaves, torn into pieces

1 tablespoon sesame seeds

1 garlic clove, crushed

½ tablespoon tomato paste

fine sea salt and freshly ground black pepper

*Pasta and rice dishes in particular often need no more than
a quick and tasty stir-fry to turn them into a meal. Simply
put the pasta or rice on to cook–prepare the vegetables and
stir-fry them. More complex stir-fry dishes involving a wide
variety of vegetables, nuts, and tofu can be added to
Chinese noodles or rice for an Oriental feast.*

1 Heat the oil in a large heavy-bottom saucepan. Sauté the
leeks, zucchini, and red pepper for about 10 minutes over a
medium heat.

2 Add the cooked pasta or rice and continue to sauté for
another 3 minutes. Stir in the basil, sesame seeds, garlic,
and tomato paste. Season to taste and serve immediately.

Serves 4

Variations:
*Try using onions or shallots, mushrooms, broccoli, peeled
and seeded tomatoes, carrots, green beans, and nuts. For
Oriental versions, add bok choy, water chestnuts,
Chinese mushrooms, bean sprouts and
5-spice powder.*

Swiss Soufflé Potatoes

4 large baking potatoes, baked and the flesh
   scooped-out

3 tablespoons finely chopped scallions

¾ cup Gruyère cheese, shredded

¾ cup Emmenthal cheese, shredded

2 garlic cloves, crushed

2 tablespoons butter

¼ cup organic whole wheat flour

½ cup whole milk

¼ cup dry white wine (optional)

3 eggs from free-range chickens, separated

1 tablespoon French mustard

pinch of freshly ground nutmeg

pinch of cayenne pepper

fine sea salt and freshly ground black pepper

1 Place the scooped-out potato flesh in a bowl. Mix in the
scallions, cheeses, and garlic.

2 Melt the butter in a pan, quickly add the flour to make a
roux. Pour in the milk gradually to make a thick white
sauce. Add the white wine and whisk it in quickly to avoid
curdling. Bring to a boil, stirring frequently, then remove
from the heat. Beat in the egg yolks, mustard, nutmeg, and
cayenne, and fold the sauce into the potato mixture.

3 Beat the egg whites in a clean, grease-free bowl until soft
peaks form. Fold carefully into the potato mixture and season. Quickly spoon the mixture back into the potato shells,
making sure they are well filled.

4 Place the potato shells on a well-oiled baking sheet and
put them quickly into a preheated oven, 325°F. Bake until
the soufflé filling is well risen and golden brown, about 30
minutes. Serve immediately.

Serves 4

Variations:

Insert wedges of cheese with tomatoes and fresh herbs into deep cuts made in the potatoes after cooking. Alternatively, try adding separately roasted vegetables such as eggplants, bell peppers, zucchini, or onions.

Ring the changes by replacing ordinary baking potatoes with sweet potatoes.

Baked Potatoes

Simple yet satisfying, baked potatoes make the perfect quick family supper as a meal in themselves or as an accompaniment to another dish. The funny thing about baked potatoes is that they are so common, common knowledge about them is assumed and so certain tips as to their preparation are being forgotten.

The best potatoes for baking are russets such as the Idaho potatoes.

Allow one large potato per person, about ½ pound (young children will probably only eat half of one). Wash and scrub the potato skins to remove any surface chemicals (if you can, buy organic potatoes—you'll never forget the flavor). Most importantly, once the potatoes are clean, dry them and prick with a fork. The oven should have been set to 400°F, at which temperature a ½ pound potato will take 50-60 minutes to cook. If you like your skins soft, rub oil into them before baking. Crisp skins are achieved by adding an extra 15 minutes to the cooking time.

To serve, cut the potatoes in half, season and fork the potato flesh a little to help it absorb the topping.

Possible toppings besides butter are sour cream with chives, shredded vegetarian cheese, cream cheese with herbs and garlic, baked beans, barbecue beans, some of the sauces on pages 101-102, or ratatouille… in fact, practically anything!

Potato Skins with Two Dips

4 large baking potatoes, scrubbed and pricked
1 tablespoon olive oil
4 tablespoons butter, melted, or a little chili oil
fine sea salt and freshly ground black pepper
KETCHUP:
1½ pounds ripe tomatoes, roughly chopped
4 tablespoons soft brown sugar
⅓ cup malt vinegar
½ teaspoon cayenne pepper
½ teaspoon paprika
1 tablespoon tomato paste
MUSTARD AND CREAM CHEESE DIP:
¾ cup sour cream or plain yogurt
½ cup cream cheese
1 tablespoon snipped fresh chives
1 tablespoon whole grain mustard, or according
    to taste

The whole family will love this. The potato skins are served with homemade ketchup and cool creamy mustard and cheese dip.

1 To make the ketchup, place the tomatoes in a large heavy-bottom saucepan. Cover and bring gently to boiling. Remove the lid and cook quickly to allow the sauce to thicken—this will take at least 40 minutes.

2 When the sauce is thick, pass it through a fine strainer and then return it to the rinsed pan. Flavor the sauce with the rest of the ingredients (the tomato paste will return the color lost in cooking).

3 Cool, cover, and refrigerate until use. (The ketchup will keep for several weeks in a clean jar with a tight-fitting lid or bottle in the refrigerator.)

4 To make the mustard and cream cheese dip, simply mix

all the ingredients together and chill well before serving.

5 Meanwhile, having brushed the potatoes well with olive oil, bake in a preheated oven, 375°F, for about 1 hour or until tender. Let cool slightly.

6 Cut each potato into 6 wedges lengthwise. Brush with melted butter or chili oil, if using for adults. Season with salt and pepper.

7 Place under a preheated broiler and broil on both sides until crisp. Serve immediately with the prepared dips.

Serves 4

Potato and Mushroom au Gratin

⅛ cup (½ stick) butter or 4 tablespoons olive oil

1 cup onions, finely sliced

1 pound leeks, thinly sliced

2 cups chestnut mushrooms, cut diagonally into
⅛-inch slices and blanched for 30 seconds

2 cups potatoes, peeled and thinly sliced

2 cups heavy cream

2 garlic cloves, crushed

⅛ teaspoon freshly ground nutmeg

½ cup Gruyère or vegetarian Cheddar cheese, shredded

fine sea salt and freshly ground black pepper

Sliced potatoes make an excellent topping for simple satisfying fare. The variations are endless but it's good to have at least one such dish up your sleeve that you know your children will enjoy.

This recipe uses cream but, if you prefer, substitute with an equal quantity of white sauce—vegans can use a white sauce made with soya milk and omit the cheese.

1 Heat the butter or olive oil in a large heavy-bottom saucepan. Add the sliced onions and cook for about 3 minutes until beginning to soften. Stir in the leeks and cook for another 5 minutes, then add the mushrooms and cook for 1 minute more.

2 Place the potatoes in a saucepan, stir in the cream, garlic, nutmeg and seasoning. Bring gently to a boil. Pour on to the onion, leek and mushroom mixture, combine well and adjust seasoning if necessary. Tip the mixture into an ovenproof shallow-sided casserole dish.

3 Place the dish in a large roasting tray half-filled with water and cook in a preheated oven, 350°F, for about 1 hour, or until tender—test with a sharp knife.

4 When the potatoes are cooked, sprinkle the top with shredded cheese and return to the oven until brown or gratinate under a preheated broiler.

Serves 4

Pastoral Pie

BASE:

¾ cup brown lentils

4 tablespoons extra-virgin olive oil

1 onion, finely sliced

2 teaspoons dried basil

1 teaspoon dried oregano

1 carrot, finely chopped

1 large red bell pepper, cored, seeded and finely chopped

1½ cups mushrooms, finely chopped

1 glass red wine or vegetable stock

1 tablespoon shoyu

1 cup tomato passata

3 garlic cloves, crushed

TOPPING:

1 pound potatoes, peeled and quartered

1 pound celeriac, quartered

1 egg, beaten (optional)

2 tablespoons butter

½ cup vegetarian hard white cheese

½ teaspoon freshly ground nutmeg

fine sea salt and freshly ground black pepper

The base of this dish is something you will use time and time again. Extremely versatile, it can go under any topping or over any pasta or rice dish; it can be added to and even taken away from; best of all, it is made from entirely natural and wholesome ingredients.

1 Soak the lentils overnight in cold water then cook in fresh water until almost mushy, drain, and set aside.

2 Heat the oil in a deep heavy-bottom saucepan. Add the onion and herbs and cook together for 5 minutes. Add the carrot and pepper and continue to cook for 5 minutes more.

3 Stir in the mushrooms and cook for yet another 5 minutes. Add the wine or stock and shoyu, cook gently to reduce the mixture by half before adding the passata, garlic, and lentils. If the mixture is a little too thick add some more wine or water. Bring to a boil and simmer, covered, for as long as possible–at least 30 minutes. When you are happy with the flavor remove half of the mixture and roughly purée it in a blender or food processor before returning it to the pan and folding it in well. Pour into a 6-cup baking dish, set aside, and prepare the topping.

4 Place the potatoes and celeriac together in a large saucepan of water and cook until tender (remember that celeriac, once peeled, will oxidize unless immersed in water). Drain and mash together. Stir in the remaining topping ingredients and season well.

5 Spread the potato and celeriac mixture over the lentil base with a spatula or else pipe it on top decoratively, using a large star nozzle. Bake in a preheated oven, 400°F, for 50-60 minutes, until the top is golden brown.

Serves 4

Variations:
There are plenty of tasty variations on the mashed potato topping. You could substitute turnips, spring greens, or even apple for the celeriac. Try adding garlic and using cream or natural yogurt for a creamier topping.

French Bread and Garlic Butter Pudding

⅓ cup extra-virgin olive oil

1 large onion, finely sliced

3 tablespoons chopped fresh basil, or
    1½ tablespoons dried basil

2 tablespoons chopped fresh parsley, or
    1-2 tablespoons dried parsley

1 large eggplant cut into 1-inch cubes

6 garlic cloves, crushed

2 red bell peppers, cored, seeded and cut into strips

2 zucchini, sliced

2 cups button mushrooms, sliced

¾ cup red wine

2 tablespoons tomato paste

½ tablespoon brown sugar

12 ounce can butter beans, drained

12 ounce can chopped tomatoes

⅓ cup pitted black olives (optional)

1 small French bread, sliced

⅛ cup Parmesan or mozzarella cheese,
    shredded (optional)

fine sea salt and freshly ground black pepper

Here is a really simple dish that all the family will enjoy. It is essentially a Mediterranean-style casserole topped with garlic bread that will tempt even the fussiest of your family. Nutritionally the dish is a perfect combination of proteins, carbohydrates, fats, and vitamins.

1 Heat 2 tablespoons of the olive oil in a large casserole dish. Add the onion and sauté for 1 minute. Season with salt and pepper and add half of the herbs, if using.

2 Add the eggplant and half of the garlic and continue to cook, stirring frequently for 5 minutes. Then add the red

peppers, zucchini, and mushrooms; cook for 1 minute until the whole dish is very hot.

3 Tip in the red wine; it should immediately hiss and start to evaporate. Cook gently to reduce it by half. Add the tomato paste, brown sugar, beans, tomatoes, olives, and the remaining herbs, if using. Stir the mixture well and bring to a gentle simmer before covering and placing in a preheated oven, 400°F, for 40 minutes.

4 While the casserole is cooking, prepare the garlic bread. Blend the remaining olive oil with the rest of the garlic. Season with salt and pepper. Brush both sides of the sliced bread with the garlic oil.

5 Take the casserole from the oven. Remove the lid and inhale deeply—the smell is wonderful! Arrange the slices of garlic bread on the top of the casserole, sprinkle with Parmesan, if using, and return to the oven, uncovered, for up to 20 minutes, or until browned and slightly crisp on top.

6 Serve with a crisp salad.

Serves 4-6

Bambeano Burgers with Garlic Focaccia

BURGERS:

¾ cup black-eyed peas

½ cup short-grain brown rice

1⅛ cups water

1½ tablespoons extra-virgin olive oil

1 large onion, finely chopped

1 green bell pepper, cored, seeded, and finely chopped

1 teaspoon ground cumin

1 teaspoon ground coriander

¼ teaspoon chili powder

1 tablespoon chopped fresh basil

1 tablespoon tomato paste

1 tablespoon shoyu

2 garlic cloves, crushed

a little organic whole wheat flour mixed with sesame

seeds, for coating

fine sea salt and freshly ground black pepper

GARLIC FOCACCIA:

4 cups unbleached bread flour

1 cake compressed yeast, blended with a little warm water and 1 teaspoon sugar

4 tablespoons olive oil, warmed, plus extra for brushing

4 garlic cloves, crushed

2 tablespoons chopped fresh oregano (optional)

coarse sea salt, for sprinkling

ITALIAN TOMATO SAUCE:

2 pounds firm ripe tomatoes, halved

¼ cup extra-virgin olive oil

1 teaspoon soft brown sugar or balsamic vinegar, to taste

This has to be the ultimate vegetarian burger recipe and will appeal to all the family, not just the children. The recipe is best made in large quantities. What is not used can be wrapped in plastic and kept frozen for up to 3 months.

I've never understood why the sesame bun is such a popular base for burgers. At best it tastes like cotton wool, at worst it is indigestible. There are so many more exciting breads to choose from. I've chosen garlic focaccia for its flavor and soft texture. Focaccia freezes well and is best made in bulk. This recipe makes 8 good-sized buns but you may well find that half a bun is all that is really needed to go with the burgers, as they are very filling.

The tomato sauce will keep refrigerated for up to a week, or can be frozen, too.

1 Cover the black-eyed peas with double their volume of cold water in a saucepan. Bring rapidly to a boil and continue boiling for 10 minutes. Remove from the heat and let cool before transferring to a plastic container. Let them soak for 12 hours or overnight. When ready to cook, return them to the saucepan with fresh water, bring to a boil, cover, and simmer for up to 1 hour or until very tender but not mushy.

2 Meanwhile, put the rice and water in a saucepan and bring to a boil. Simmer, covered, for up to 45 minutes, or until cooked.

3 Heat 1 tablespoon of the olive oil in a large skillet. Add the onion, green pepper, and spices, and stir fry until the onions begin to soften. Stir in the basil, tomato paste, shoyu, and garlic, and cook for 1 minute further.

4 Combine the cooled, cooked black-eyed peas and rice in a blender or food processor. Add the vegetable mixture to this and blend it all together for a few seconds. Judge the texture according to your own preference–some may like it coarser than others. Adjust the seasoning. Divide the mixture into 8 and shape into burgers. Brush with the remaining olive oil and roll in the flour and sesame seed mixture. Chill the burgers - overnight if possible–before shallow frying for 5 minutes on each side.

5 Mix ½ cup of the flour with the yeast liquid in a clean bowl and let rise for 30 minutes in a warm, draft-free place, covered with a damp dishcloth.

6 Knead the remaining flour into the frothing yeast, add the warmed olive oil, the garlic, and oregano, if you're using, as you knead the dough. Leave the dough to rise as before in a draft-free place for 1 hour, or until doubled in bulk.

7 Knock the dough back and divide into 8. Knead each piece briefly and shape into a flat bun shape. Brush with olive oil and sprinkle with coarse salt, then bake in a preheated oven, 400°F, for 15 minutes. Let cool before using.

8 To make the sauce, place the tomatoes in a saucepan with the olive oil. Cook for about 8 minutes, stirring frequently, then rub the mixture through a fine strainer. Adjust the flavor as you wish. If the tomatoes are very sweet add a little balsamic vinegar; if slightly bitter add soft brown sugar and season with salt and pepper.

9 To serve the burgers, cut the buns in half, toast briefly, top with a burger, a little tomato sauce, and serve with a salad. If you like, spread the buns with a mixture of mayonnaise and mustard, and add a few slices of onion and tomato. Spread the burgers with French or German mustard, top with mozzarella cheese and broil until bubbling.

Makes 8

Leek and Dolcelatte Risotto

⅓ cup (¾ stick) unsalted butter

5 leeks, white parts only, cut into ¼-inch thick slices

2 teaspoons dried thyme

¾ cup ceps, sliced

6 sun-dried tomatoes, sliced

2-3 garlic cloves, crushed

1½ cups dolcelatte, Gorgonzola or Stilton cheese, crumbled

2 onions, finely sliced

2 cups arborio rice

2 cups dry white wine

4 cups hot vegetable stock

fine sea salt and freshly ground black pepper

To serve:

4 tablespoons chopped fresh parsley or cilantro

¾ cup Grana Padano or Parmesan cheese, shredded

Arborio rice is necessary for this dish. The risotto is cooked by the absorption method and arborio grains absorb well without losing their shape or sticking together. A good risotto should always look creamy and the rice should be al dente, not overcooked.

1 Melt 3 tablespoons of the butter in a large skillet. Add the leeks and thyme and stir-fry gently for 10 minutes; the leeks should retain a lot of bite. Stir in the sliced ceps, tomatoes, garlic, and dolcelatte. Allow the dolcelatte to melt over a very low heat; if it gets too hot, remove from the heat.

2 In a large saucepan heat the rest of the butter, add the onions and stir-fry for 3 minutes. Add the rice and make sure it is well coated by the butter; add a little more butter if necessary. When the rice is very hot, pour in 1 cup of the wine, which will be absorbed very quickly, then add the

rest. When this has been absorbed start adding the hot vegetable stock, a ladleful at a time.

3 When the rice is just cooked, about 15 minutes, stir in the cheese mixture and cook for a further 2 minutes before serving. Season to taste and serve, garnished with chopped parsley or cilantro and shredded cheese, accompanied by a fresh leafy salad.

Serves 4-6

Rigatoni with Cheesy Sun-dried Tomato Sauce

1 tablespoon extra-virgin olive oil

1 large onion, finely sliced

1 small bulb of fennel, finely sliced

1 yellow bell pepper, cored, seeded, and finely sliced

1 fresh red chili, seeded and finely chopped

2 garlic cloves, crushed

1 tablespoon balsamic vinegar

1 teaspoon soft brown sugar

2 tablespoons tomato paste

12 ounce can chopped tomatoes

1⅛ cup red wine

¼ cup sun-dried tomatoes in oil, chopped

1 bunch of basil, chopped

4 cups dried rigatoni

1¼ cups mozzarella cheese, shredded

¼ cup pine nuts, toasted

fine sea salt and freshly ground black pepper

TO GARNISH:

1 sprig of mint or basil

a little shredded vegetarian Pecorino cheese

This delicious sauce is definitely best made a day in advance.

1 Heat the oil in a large heavy-bottom saucepan. Add the onion, fennel, yellow pepper, and chili, and stir fry gently until the onion begins to soften. Increase the heat and add the garlic, balsamic vinegar, and soft brown sugar, stirring continuously. Reduce the vinegar by half, then stir in the tomato paste, canned tomatoes, and wine. Let simmer, covered, for 20 minutes.

2 Remove from the stove, cool slightly, and purée in a blender or food processor, or rub through a strainer. Tip into a clean container and add the sun-dried tomatoes and basil. Let their flavors infuse as the sauce cools down. At this stage it's a good idea to keep the sauce covered in a refrigerator overnight.

3 Fifteen minutes before you are ready to eat, cook the rigatoni according to the package instructions in plenty of boiling water. Re-heat the sauce and when hot stir in the mozzarella. Adjust the seasoning to taste.

4 Drain the pasta and tip into a warmed serving dish (it's a nice touch to rub the dish with a little garlic and olive oil first). Pour the sauce over the pasta, sprinkle with toasted pine nuts, and garnish with sprigs of fresh mint or basil and shredded Pecorino.

5 Serve immediately, accompanied by warm Italian bread and a fresh, herby green salad.

Serves 4

Tamale Pie

lentil base (see below)

TOPPING:

1 cup fine corn meal

1 tablespoon unbleached all-purpose white flour

½ teaspoon salt

2 teaspoons baking powder

1 egg (large) from a free-range chicken, beaten

⅓ cup whole milk

1 tablespoon extra-virgin olive oil

chopped fresh cilantro, for garnish

Using the basic lentil base from the recipe for Pastoral Pie (see page 107) with the addition of 1 seeded green chili and a 12 ounce can of red kidney beans, rinsed, and drained, try this topping to make a delicious Mexican-style pie.

1 Pour the lentil base mixture into a lightly greased 7-inch diameter baking dish.

2 Mix all the dry topping ingredients together. Stir in the egg, milk, and olive oil, and mix well. Spoon the mixture over the lentil base, then place in a preheated oven, 425°F, and bake for 20-25 minutes, or until firm to the touch. Garnish with chopped cilantro and serve immediately.

Serves 4

Thai Roast Tofu and Rice Noodles

8 ounces firm tofu, cubed

3 tablespoons shoyu

2 tablespoons sweet sherry, or dry sherry plus
    1 tablespoon soft brown sugar

1 tablespoon mirin, a sweet Japanese cooking rice
    wine

1 tablespoon plus 2 teaspoons sesame oil

4 garlic cloves, crushed

1 teaspoon Szechuan chili powder

1-inch piece of fresh ginger root, shredded

4 cups dried rice noodles

4 scallions, cut into 1-inch lengths

2 cups broccoli flowerets

2 cups shiitake mushrooms, halved or
    left whole

4 cups bean sprouts

4 tablespoons smooth peanut butter

¼ cup roasted peanuts, chopped

Here is a simple dinner dish that uses basic ingredients to good effect. Tofu and rice noodles are both easily available from most Chinese supermarkets.

1 Place the tofu in a dish. Blend the shoyu, sherry, and mirin with 2 teaspoons of the sesame oil and 2 cloves of garlic, chili powder, and the ginger. Pour this mixture over the top of the tofu and leave to marinate for 3 hours.

2 Meanwhile, cook the noodles in plenty of boiling water according to the package instructions. Drain, cool, and set aside in enough cold water to cover them (they can be kept in the refrigerator like this for several days).

3 30 minutes before eating, remove the tofu from the marinade—reserving the marinade—and place in a dish. Roast in a preheated oven, 400°F, for 25 minutes, then set aside.

4 In a large heavy skillet or wok, heat the remaining 1 tablespoon of sesame oil. Stir-fry the scallions with the broccoli flowerets for approximately 3 minutes. Add the mushrooms and continue to cook for a further 2 minutes. Add the remaining garlic and the bean sprouts, and stir-fry for 1 minute more. Stir in the peanut butter, and when it is really hot, add the reserved marinade. The sauce should instantly thicken—if it becomes too thick, add a little water and adjust the seasoning accordingly.

5 Lastly, toss in the cooked noodles, roasted peanuts, and the roasted tofu, and heat through thoroughly before serving immediately on its own or with a light salad.

Serves 4-6

Chestnut Mushroom and Shallot Steamed Pudding

FILLING:

⅛ cup (½ stick) butter, or 4 tablespoons olive oil

1 cup shallots, chopped

1 carrot, chopped, or 3 baby carrots, halved

1 celery stalk, roughly chopped

1 small swede turnip, topped, tailed, peeled, and chopped

2 teaspoons dried thyme

2 garlic cloves, crushed

4 tablespoons unbleached all-purpose white flour

2 cups red wine or vegetable stock

2 teaspoons freshly grated horseradish (optional)

1 tablespoon whole grain mustard

4 tablespoons chopped fresh parsley

12 chestnuts, cooked and halved

2½ cups small chestnut or button mushrooms

fine sea salt and freshly ground black pepper

PUDDING:

3 cups unbleached all-purpose white flour

1-2 teaspoons salt

½ teaspoon baking powder

¾ cup shredded vegetable suet

¾ cup cold water

shredded rind of 1 lemon

butter or vegan margarine, for greasing

1 tablespoon finely chopped fresh cilantro or parsley, for garnish

This dish is the perfect foil for a cold winter's evening. The filling is best made 1-2 days in advance to allow the flavors to mingle.

1 To make the filling, heat the butter or oil in a large, heavy-bottom saucepan. Add the shallots, and fry, covered, for 3 minutes. Add the carrots, celery, swede, and thyme, and continue to cook, covered, for 5 minutes.

2 Stir in the garlic, then add the flour, and mix in evenly. When the whole mixture is very hot, pour in the red wine or stock, gradually letting it thicken and come to a boil. When all the liquid has evaporated, reduce the heat and let the sauce simmer. Add the horseradish, mustard, parsley, salt, and pepper.

3 Finally add the mushrooms and cook for 2 minutes (they must not be well cooked as they still have to survive 1-1½ hours in the steamer). Set aside to cool.

4 To make the pudding, mix the flour, salt, baking powder, and vegetable suet in a bowl. Bind together with the water and knead lightly until smooth. Roll out to a round 13-inches in diameter. Cut a quarter out of the circle and use the larger piece to line a greased 6-cup ovenproof bowl. Wet the overlap with water to seal the join.

5 Pour the filling into the lined bowl.

6 Re-roll the remaining quarter of pastry into a circle to fit the top of the pudding basin. Dampen the edges with water and seal all around the edges.

7 Place a sheet of wax paper and a piece of similarly sized foil over the top of the bowl and secure with string as tightly as possible. Stand the bowl on a heatproof saucer in the bottom of a large boiling pan. Fill the pan with enough boiling water to come about halfway up the side of the ovenproof bowl. Cover the saucepan and boil for 1½ hours. Alternatively, place the ovenproof bowl in an ovenproof dish or roasting pan, pour in enough water to come halfway up the side of the basin and cook in the middle of a hot oven, 400°F, for 1½ hours.

8 To serve, carefully run a spatula around the ovenproof bowl, gently easing the pudding away from the sides. Place a serving dish over the top of the bowl and, holding firmly, invert it. The pudding should slip out easily. Garnish with chopped parsley or cilantro and serve.

Serves 4-6

Dutch Crêpe Stack

1 tablespoon olive oil

2 green bell peppers, cored, seeded, and cut into small strips

2 yellow bell peppers, cored, seeded, and cut into small strips

4 small zucchini, diagonally sliced

2 cups chestnut mushrooms, sliced

2 tablespoons chopped fresh basil

2 cups vegetarian Cheddar or mozzarella cheese, shredded

fine sea salt and freshly ground black pepper

CREPES:

1½ cups organic whole wheat flour

2 teaspoons baking powder

1 teaspoon chopped fresh dill

½ cup whole milk

⅓ cup cold water

¼ cup sour cream

2 eggs (small) from free-range chickens, beaten

butter, for cooking

TOMATO SAUCE:

3 tablespoons olive oil

1 large red onion, finely chopped

1 teaspoon paprika

1 tablespoon red wine vinegar

1 tablespoon soft brown sugar

1 tablespoon tomato paste

12 ounce can chopped tomatoes

¾ cup red wine

2 garlic cloves, crushed

MUSHROOM AND TARRAGON SAUCE:

¼ cup (½ stick) butter

3 shallots, finely chopped

3 cups flat mushrooms, chopped

½ teaspoon ground coriander

1 cup sour or light cream

½ tablespoon chopped fresh tarragon, or
   ¼ tablespoon dried tarragon

dash of shoyu, to taste

A stack of crêpes layered with succulent vegetables and a tasty sauce, this is a recipe guaranteed to appeal to everyone in the family, even the baby. It looks and tastes great, and is still unusual enough to hook the children.

The crêpes are a little more robust than normal as the recipe requires them to have some structural properties. They may be prepared up to a day in advance.

1 To make the crêpes, combine the flour, baking powder, and dill in a bowl. Blend all the liquid ingredients together, then add them gradually to the flour, stirring all the time. Add salt and pepper if you wish, then set the batter aside. (Crêpe batter improves with age, so if you can, make it well in advance and store in the refrigerator. When ready to use, beat the batter and add a little more water if necessary.)

2 To make the tomato sauce, heat the oil in a deep, heavy-bottom saucepan, add the onion, paprika, and salt and pepper.

Sauté until the onion begins to soften, add the vinegar and sugar, and heat gently to reduce by half. Stir in the tomato paste, the tomatoes, and the red wine, bring to a boil and simmer for at least 30 minutes. Add the garlic and adjust the seasoning to taste. Let cool and then store, covered, in the refrigerator.

3 For the mushroom sauce, melt the butter in a heavy-bottom saucepan, add the shallots, and sauté for about 3 minutes. Stir in the mushrooms and coriander and continue to cook for another 10 minutes over a medium heat. Pour in the cream and tarragon and gently bring back to a boil. Allow the sauce to bubble for a few minutes until the cream has reduced and thickened. Adjust the seasoning to taste and add a dash of shoyu.

4 For the vegetables, simply stir-fry them in the olive oil to the state which you like, or roast them in the oven. However you cook them, add the basil and seasoning right at the end and reserve the cheese.

5 To cook the crêpes, heat a little butter in a 9-inch crêpe pan or skillet. Make sure that the bottom is well covered by the butter. When hot, spoon in about 3 tablespoons of the crêpe batter–enough to amply cover the bottom of the pan. Reduce the heat a little and cook for 3-4 minutes until bubbles appear on the surface. Turn the crêpe over and cook the other side for 1-2 minutes only.

6 Remove the crêpe from the pan and place on absorbent paper towels. Repeat until you have 4 or 5 good crêpes. Keep any leftover batter for the next day.

7 To assemble the crêpe stack, brush an ovenproof dish with melted butter. Place a crêpe in the dish and cover with 1-2 tablespoons of tomato sauce. Add one-quarter of the vegetable mixture and top with the shredded cheese. Make sure you spread an equal amount of vegetable mixture around the rim of the crêpes as in the middle so that the stack doesn't dip around the sides. Cover with the next crêpe and repeat the process until all the crêpes, tomato sauce, vegetables, and cheese are used up. You now have

a very funny-looking "cake" topped with cheese.

8 Place in a preheated oven, 400°F, and cook for 35-40 minutes or until golden and bubbling. Meanwhile, re-heat the mushroom sauce.

9 To serve, cut the crêpe stack into wedges. Garnish with chopped parsley and serve with the mushroom sauce.

Serves 4

Red Bell Pepper and Corn Fritters with Tangy Mustard Sauce

FRITTERS:

½ cup extra-virgin olive oil

1 onion, finely chopped

3 red bell peppers, cored, seeded, and finely chopped

1 cup frozen corn, drained

2 cups organic whole wheat flour

2 teaspoons baking powder

1 teaspoon dry mustard powder

½ teaspoon ground nutmeg

3 tablespoons finely chopped fresh parsley

2 eggs from free-range chickens, separated

1 cup whole milk

oil, for cooking

SAUCE:

½ cup sour cream

2 tablespoons snipped fresh chives

½ tablespoon clear honey or mango chutney

fine sea salt and freshly ground black pepper

Anything that involves crêpe batter and a skillet is bound to

120

be popular with the children. This is the sort of dish that comes into the category of "special occasion or treat." Do not serve more than once a month, although the children will want it all the time. Serve as a side dish for a wonderful accompaniment to roasts at more adult affairs.

1 To make the fritters, heat 3 tablespoons of the olive oil in a large heavy-botom skillet. Sauté the onion for 3 minutes, then add the red peppers and continue to sauté for 5 minutes. Stir in the corn, season, and set aside to cool.

2 Sift together in a bowl the flour, the baking powder, and ¼ teaspoon each of salt and pepper. Stir in the mustard powder, nutmeg, and parsley and make a well in the center.

3 Beat the egg yolks and milk together and pour this into the middle of the dry ingredients. Incorporate the liquid well to make a batter, then add the cooled vegetables.

4 Finally, beat the egg whites until stiff but not over-stiff, and fold them carefully into the batter until well combined.

5 Heat a little oil in a large skillet. Drop 1 good tablespoon of the batter into the pan and, depending on the size of the pan, make anything up to 6 fritters per person. Cook until golden brown–about 30 seconds each side. Keep warm in a low oven on a lightly buttered serving dish until all the fritters are cooked.

6 To make the mustard sauce, combine all the ingredients together in a small bowl.

7 Serve the fritters immediately with a salad or lightly steamed vegetables and the mustard sauce. Alternatively, serve with ketchup (see page 106).

Serves 4

Lone Star Mushroom Nuggets with Campfire Sauce

SAUCE:

1 tablespoon vegetable oil

2 onions, finely chopped

½ teaspoon chili powder

3 garlic cloves, crushed

1½ cups Ketchup (see page 106)

¼ cup vegetarian Worcestershire sauce

1½ tablespoons molasses

⅓ cup water

MUSHROOMS:

34 chestnut mushrooms, stalks carefully removed

1 cup garlic and herb-flavored cream cheese

⅓ cup organic whole wheat flour

2 eggs from free-range chickens, beaten

¼ cup whole milk

1 cup organic whole wheat bread crumbs,
    seasoned

oil, for cooking

I have never been a great consumer or preparer of deep-fried foods, but if it is done infrequently it is something for you and your family to look forward to. In this recipe stuffed mushrooms are coated in bread crumbs, fried, and served with a wonderful sauce. Mushroom nuggets freeze well and cook from frozen. Vegans can use a dairy-free pakora batter and fill their mushrooms with a mushroom sauce.

1 Make the sauce by heating the oil in a saucepan. Add the onions, chili powder, and garlic, and sauté until beginning to soften. Add the rest of the ingredients, bring to a boil and then simmer for 5 minutes.

2 Meanwhile, fill each mushroom with cream cheese. Combine the flour, eggs, and milk in a bowl to make a smooth batter. Dip the mushrooms into the batter and then quickly in the seasoned bread crumbs. Deep-fry the mushrooms until golden brown, about 5 minutes, and serve with the sauce.

Serves 4

Calzone Carciofi

PIZZA DOUGH:

2½ cups unbleached bread flour, plus extra for sprinkling

1 cake compressed fresh yeast

1 teaspoon soft brown sugar

¾ cup tepid water

2 tablespoons extra-virgin olive oil,
    plus extra for brushing

FILLING AND SAUCE:

4 tablespoons extra-virgin olive oil

2 garlic cloves, crushed

12 ounce can chopped tomatoes, or
    1 pound fresh tomatoes

10 basil leaves, torn into pieces

3 cups mozzarella cheese, cubed

6 artichoke hearts, preserved in olive oil and
    halved horizontally

1½ cups button mushrooms, sliced

fine sea salt and freshly ground black pepper

I was amazed to discover that our children loved artichoke hearts. This discovery was in France, at a time of year when you could stagger back from the market, your traditional carrier bag simply bursting with inexpensive globe artichokes. I thought it would be nice to include them here, although mushrooms, asparagus, or indeed any favorite pizza topping can be substituted. Calzone are excellent dinner candidates because they can be totally prepared and par-cooked earlier in the day, then finished off when the hoards arrive home to eat.

1 For the pizza dough, as for making bread of any kind, try to ensure that all the equipment used is warm. Mix the flour and 1 teaspoon salt together in a large bowl. Pour some of the tepid water into a small jug. Crumble in the yeast and sugar. Cover and leave for 10 minutes in a warm place until foaming.

2 Make a well in the flour and pour in the yeast mixture and the oil. Mix until the water is incorporated. The dough should be smooth and pliable and readily leave the sides of the bowl. If it is too dry add more water. Knead the dough on a lightly floured surface. When soft and elastic it is ready; this will take 10 minutes.

3 Oil a bowl and add the ball of dough, score its surface with a knife to help it rise, and lightly sprinkle with a little flour. Cover the bowl with a damp dishcloth and put in a warm, draft-free place to double in size. This will take at least 1 hour.

4 Meanwhile, to make the filling and the sauce, gently heat the olive oil in a large saucepan. Add the garlic and a little seasoning and cook it without coloring. After about 1 minute add the tomatoes. Cook, taking care not to allow burning, for at least 10 minutes to reduce the canned tomato liquid slightly. Add the basil, season, and set aside. (This sauce is best cooked well ahead of the time of serving.)

5 When the dough is ready, knock it back with your fist, then knead for 3 minutes before dividing into 12 equal balls. Flatten each ball with the palm of your hand, then either roll or press each into a 4-inch round, about ⅛-inch thick. Brush each circle on both sides with extra-virgin olive oil.

6 Spread ½ a tablespoon of the sauce on each circle, taking care not to get it too close to the edge. Arrange half an artichoke heart and some mushrooms on the top of each, with cubes of mozzarella. Take care to arrange the vegetables and cheese on one half of each circle only.

7 Fold over the other half of the circle and pinch the edges together to form a half-moon shape. Sprinkle with flour (or corn meal, if preferred) and place on a floured baking sheet. Bake in a preheated oven, 425°F, for 20 minutes, or until golden brown.

8 Serve with the remaining sauce and a crisp salad.

Makes 12 x 4-inch, or 2 x 11-inch calzone

Hot Lentil and Cheddar Cheese Salad

1 cup lentils, washed

6 cups water

3 garlic cloves, crushed

1 bouquet garni

1 carrot, peeled and chopped

3 shallots, finely chopped

fine sea salt and freshly ground black pepper

DRESSING:

½ cup extra-virgin olive oil

2 tablespoons balsamic vinegar

1 tablespoon Dijon mustard

3 garlic cloves, crushed

1 tablespoon snipped fresh chives

2 teaspoons chopped fresh chervil

SALAD BASE:

½ pound fresh ripe tomatoes, peeled, seeded, and
    chopped

1 bunch of scallions, chopped

2 gem lettuces, pulled apart

2 red bell peppers, cored, seeded, roasted, and
    torn into strips

½ curly endive, roasted, and torn into strips

½ lettuce, roasted, and torn into strips

2 cups Cheddar cheese, cut into ½-inch cubes

1 tablespoon chopped fresh parsley

12 ripe black olives, for garnish (optional)

This salad is a wholesome meal in itself and a swift but unusual answer to a family's needs at the end of the day. Puy lentils are truly king among lentils, but they do require careful washing. This salad contains everything a growing family could possibly want and vegans can substitute cubes

of pan-fried tofu for the cheese.

1 There is no need to soak the lentils overnight, but rinse and drain them thoroughly. Place in a large saucepan with the water, garlic, bouquet garni, carrot, shallots, and season with salt and pepper to taste. Bring to a boil, then simmer until tender, about 40 minutes.

2 While the lentils are cooking, combine all the dressing ingredients thoroughly and assemble the salad base without the cheese or tofu, if using, and parsley in a salad bowl.

3 When the lentils are cooked add three-quarters of the dressing, the cheese, and the parsley to them. Pour the rest of the dressing over the salad in the bowl then top this with the lentils. Garnish with black olives and serve.

Serves 4

Family Stew and Dumplings

1 cup dried mixed beans (butter beans,
    kidney beans, flageolets, or borlotti beans)

1 tablespoon extra-virgin olive oil

1 large onion, finely sliced

1 large leek, finely sliced

1 cup carrots, chopped

½ cup celeriac, chopped

½ cup parsnip, chopped

1 red bell pepper, cored, seeded, and cut into strips

1 cup mushrooms, sliced

1 dessertspoon soft brown sugar

1 dessertspoon red wine vinegar

12 ounce can chopped tomatoes

1 tablespoon tomato paste

1 teaspoon yeast extract, dissolved in
    1 cup boiling water

2 tablespoons torn basil leaves

1 bay leaf

DUMPLINGS:

¾ cup self-rising flour

½ teaspoon salt

2 tablespoons vegetarian suet

⅛ cup vegetarian Cheddar cheese, shredded

1 tablespoon chopped fresh parsley

1 tablespoon chopped fresh thyme

fine sea salt and freshly ground black pepper

Family stews tend to evolve; look at this as a starter recipe and see how yours develops over the years. Family stews can be topped with a wide range of toppings—here I've chosen dumplings.

1 Soak the mixed beans overnight. Boil them rapidly in fresh water for about 10 minutes, then simmer until tender, about 50-60 minutes. Drain the beans well.

2 Heat the oil in a large casserole dish. Add the onion and leek and cook for 3 minutes. Add the rest of the vegetables except the mushrooms, and cook for a further 5 minutes. Add the mushrooms, sugar, and wine vinegar, simmer gently, and reduce the liquid by half.

3 Stir in the tomatoes and tomato paste and bring to a boil. Add the beans and the water and bring the casserole to a gentle simmer before stirring in the basil and bay leaf, and season to taste.

4 Cover the casserole, transfer to a preheated oven, 350°F, for at least 1 hour.

5 Meanwhile, make the dumplings. Combine the flour and salt together in a bowl, then rub in the suet until the mixture resembles breadcrumbs. Add enough cold water to form a firm dough.

6 Knead the shredded cheese, fresh herbs, and seasoning into the dough, then break into pieces and form into walnut-sized dumplings.

7 When the stew has been in the oven for 40 minutes remove it and dot the surface with the dumplings. Replace the lid and allow the stew to cook for at least a further 20 minutes. Serve hot.

Serves 4

EVERYDAY DESSERTS

On good days everyday desserts follow everyday dinners. Here are several simple desserts that you can make very quickly. My wife, Kate, has a very sweet tooth and for her no meal is complete without something sweet to round it off—even savory toast has to be followed by a ripe peach or apricot!

Cold Chocolate Fondue

CHOCOLATE SAUCE:

½ cup good-quality dark or white chocolate, broken into pieces

¾ cup light cream, or water if vegan

1½ tablespoons soft brown sugar

FRUIT:

1 cup fresh strawberries, hulled

1 cup fresh pineapple, cubed

1 cup ripe nectarines, cut into wedges

1 cup fresh cherries, pitted

1 cup Cantaloupe melon, cubed

1 cup seedless grapes

3 tablespoons lemon juice

This is a simple and popular way of serving a fruit salad. Only use chocolate containing more than 35% cocoa solids. For a dinner party add a little kirsch or schnapps to the chocolate sauce, if you like.

1 To make the chocolate sauce, melt the chocolate in a bowl set over a saucepan of boiling water. Add the sugar to the melted chocolate. Let cool for 5 minutes, then stir in the cream or water.

2 To serve, equip the family with toothpicks, a bowl of sauce, and the freshly prepared fruit, and see it disappear! Small chewy meringues are excellent accompaniments.

Serves 4

Strawberry Ice Cream

2 cups rhubarb, trimmed and chopped

2 cups fresh strawberries, hulled and chopped

¼ cup soft brown sugar

juice of 2 oranges, at least ½ cup

1 teaspoon ground ginger

12 ounce can evaporated milk

3 cups plain yogurt

As a popular dessert, nothing is quicker than ice cream, so why not have a go at making your own? Allow 20 minutes for defrosting once it is out of the freezer.

1 Place the chopped fruit, sugar, orange juice, and ground ginger in a large heavy saucepan, bring to a boil, and then simmer until very tender, stirring occasionally, for 10 minutes. Remove the pan from the heat and let cool, then blend in a blender or food processor until really smooth. Alternatively, rub through a strainer.

2 Stir in the evaporated milk and yogurt, mixing well to form a good smooth texture. Pour the mixture into a shallow plastic freezer container and place in the freezer. Stir vigorously every 30 minutes while it is freezing.

3 When totally frozen, wrap in plastic wrap and keep frozen until needed.

Serves 4

Quick Raspberry and Ginger Cheesecake

BASE:

½ cup (1 stick) unsalted butter, melted then cooled

2 cups ginger cookies, crushed

FILLING:

½ cup heavy cream

1 cup mascarpone cheese

2 tablespoons clear honey

juice of 1 lime

3 cups raspberries or strawberries

One thing that really annoys me is cheesecakes set with gelatin or agar agar. What a ghastly substance to combine with succulent fruit and fresh dairy produce! Baked cheesecakes I find a bit on the dry side—I like cheesecake to be firm but moist and to taste all the way through like this one.

1 Make the base by combining the melted butter and the crushed cookies and pressing them into a greased 8-inch quiche pan with a removable bottom. Chill for at least 30 minutes.

2 For the filling, whip the cream in a bowl until firm but not stiff, then add the mascarpone, beating it into the cream to a smooth texture. Fold in the honey and lime juice and most of the raspberries or strawberries, reserving a few for decoration.

3 Spoon the cheese mixture onto the chilled cookie base and smooth the surface over with a spatula. Chill for at least 3 hours and just before serving decorate with the reserved raspberries.

Serves 4

Pear and Banana Scotch Pancakes

8 Scotch pancakes or drop biscuits

2 tablespoons unsalted butter

2 pears, peeled, cored, and quartered

2 teaspoons ground cinnamon

2 tablespoons clear honey

juice of ½ orange

3 tablespoons lemon juice

2 bananas, halved lengthwise then halved across
   widthways

4 tablespoons heavy cream or sour cream

Good-quality Scotch pancakes or drop biscuits go very well with quickly cooked seasonal fruits.

1 Melt the butter in a large skillet. Add the pears and cinnamon and cook gently for 4 minutes. Stir in the honey, orange, and lemon juice and bananas, and cook for a further 5 minutes.

2 Meanwhile, toast the Scotch pancakes or biscuits under a pre-heated broiler, allowing 2 per person. When ready, place on warmed plates topped with the fruit and a spoonful of yogurt or heavy cream.

Serves 4

Banoffee Crumble Cake

BASE:

12 ounce can evaporated milk, unopened

1 cup sweet shortcrust dough,
   chilled (see page 130)

3 large bananas, sliced and dipped in lemon juice
   and water

TOPPING:

½ cup (1 stick) unsalted butter

1 cup organic whole wheat flour

½ cup soft brown sugar

½ cup regular oats

½ cup mixed chopped nuts

1 teaspoon ground mixed spice

Here's a variation on Banoffee Pie which is good hot or cold, and excellent served with fresh custard or cream.

1 Make the toffee well in advance by boiling the unopened can of evaporated milk in a saucepan of water for 3 hours, remembering to keep the water topped up. Remove the can from the water and let cool slightly before opening carefully. The evaporated milk will have become a thick caramel-colored toffee.

2 Roll out the chilled dough using very little excess flour. Try to only roll in one direction, until it is about ⅛-inch thick.

3 Lightly brush a 9-inch quiche pan with oil and line it with the dough, trimming off any excess. Prick the bottom with a fork. Line the dough with wax paper and fill with baking beans—ceramic ones if possible. Place in a preheated oven, 375°F, for about 10 minutes or until the dough is just beginning to color. Remove the baking beans and let the pie cool.

4 Meanwhile, to make the topping, rub the butter into the flour in a bowl until it resembles fine bread crumbs, then stir in the rest of the ingredients.

5 Line the par-cooked pie shell with the sliced bananas and top with the toffee. Sprinkle the crumb topping over this and lightly smooth all over. Return the pie to the oven and bake for 20-25 minutes until golden brown.

6 Serve with heavy cream.

Serves 4

Sweet Shortcrust Dough

1 cup organic whole wheat flour, sift but retain bran

pinch of salt

¼ cup soft brown sugar

¼ cup (½ stick) unsalted butter or vegan margarine at room temperature

2 egg yolks from free-range chicken eggs–vegans can use 3 tablespoons soya flour, plus more water

There are many variations of this recipe, but few use organic whole wheat flour. The technique of sifting out the bran and adding it back later on is one which will hold good for almost all forms of dough, bread, and cake making.

1 Sift the flour and salt onto a clean, cold surface (marble is best). Make a well in the center. Add the sugar, butter, egg yolks, and bran, if using. Using your fingertips, work the ingredients together until they are well mixed to form a soft but not sticky dough. It may be necessary to add a little water; it definitely will be if you're making the bran version.

Makes enough for a 9-inch pie pan

Tofu and Blueberry Brûlée

1 tablespoon kirsch (optional)

2 cups fresh or thawed frozen blueberries

8 ounces silken tofu

1 tablespoon maple syrup

½ teaspoon vanilla extract

½ cup mixed nuts, lightly toasted

½ cup soft brown sugar

This dish is equally good for vegans and will cook well using any soft fruit or even poached hard fruit.

If using the kirsch, which adults particularly will enjoy, marinate half of blueberries in the kirsch.

1 Blend the tofu, the maple syrup, vanilla extract, and 1 cup of the plain blueberries in a bowl until smooth.

2 Reserve 8 of the remaining blueberries, whether marinated or not, and divide the rest among 4 ramekins. Top with the smooth tofu mixture. Sprinkle with the toasted mixed nuts and chill well for about 1 hour.

3 Meanwhile, melt the sugar in a small heavy-bottom saucepan. When dissolved and a caramel color, pour a thin layer on the top of each ramekin. Chill again for 1 hour.

4 Serve, decorated with the reserved blueberries.

Serves 4

Rhubarb, Gooseberry, and Lemon Steamed Pudding

FILLING:

1 cup soft brown sugar, according to taste

1 cup water

1½ pounds fresh gooseberries, topped and tailed

shredded rind and juice of 1 lemon

SPONGE:

½ cup (1 stick) unsalted butter

½ cup soft brown sugar

½ teaspoon vanilla extract

2 eggs from free-range chickens, beaten

1 egg yolk from a free-range chicken

1½ cups self-rising flour

juice and finely shredded rind of ½ lemon

After a very simple main course it's always nice to stun the family by magically producing a steamed dessert. Steamed desserts are generally made during winter months with winter fruit such as apples and pears, but I've never known anyone turn one down even in midsummer! Frozen gooseberries and almost any other fruit can be substituted for the fresh gooseberries.

If you have a microwave this is a truly instant dessert. Use 2 ovenproof bowls or halve the ingredients. They will only take 5-8 minutes to cook on a High setting, depending on the power of your machine.

1 Boil the sugar and water together in a heavy saucepan to make a syrup. Add the gooseberries and poach them gently until tender but not mushy. Set aside.

2 Half-fill a large saucepan with water and bring to a boil. Grease a 3-cup ovenproof bowl with butter.

3 Cream the butter and sugar together in a bowl until light and fluffy in texture. Add the vanilla extract, then gradually beat in the eggs and egg yolk.

4 Using a metal spoon, carefully fold in the flour, the lemon juice, and rind.

5 Spoon most of the gooseberries into the prepared ovenproof bowl, then cover with the sponge mixture—there should be enough to come three-quarters of the way up the sides of the bowl.

6 Cover the bowl with buttered foil and secure with string. Place in the pan of boiling water. Reduce the heat to a simmer. Cover and cook for 1½ hours.

7 When cooked, invert the pudding onto a plate and spoon any excess gooseberry "syrup" over it. Serve with cream, yogurt or real custard.

Serves 4

FAMILY FEASTS

Traditional family feasts tend to center on a prized "lump" of meat. How many times do you hear people boasting about their holiday turkey: "it was huge, you should have seen it!"–almost as if they had reared the animal themselves. Not wanting to feel left out, vegetarians have devised similar "lumps" for themselves like nut roast, with which you can have all the trimmings.

In this chapter we have "feasts" in the true spirit of the family. Feasts which all the family share, both physically and socially. These feasts are for conversing over and for enjoying each other's company. By necessity they are flexible feasts, easily expanded upon, and some can expand outdoors into the garden.

Of all the countries in the world, England seems to be forgetting its family feasts. Only 20 miles across the English Channel, family eating is still the very cornerstone of society. In France the family includes not only Mom, Dad and 2.4 children, but also grandparents, aunts, uncles, cousins, good friends, and sometimes people just passing by. Most families get together, if not daily, then certainly weekly; food is shared and problems discussed. Where have we gone wrong? Throughout the world families are eating together–one can instantly name Italians, Indians, Chinese, Spanish, and Liverpudlians, so what's happened to us? At the end of the day we are too busy. Even if it's only once a week, get your family together–if you haven't got family get friends–communication is vital for our society.

FEAST ONE

The riot of color, texture, and taste of Mexican food occurred when the Spanish cookery culture imposed itself on the tranquil but refined tastes of a highly developed Indian culture in South America.

Today Mexican food is becoming more and more popular, especially as family food. Avoid using hot chiles; there are plenty of cool ones to choose from!

Serves 4

Mexican Fajitas and Frijoles
Tomato and Cilantro Salsa

Tijuana Fruit Salsa

Mexican Fajitas and Frijoles

FLOUR TORTILLAS:

2½ cups unbleached all-purpose white flour

1 teaspoon fine sea salt

¼ cup white vegetable fat

½ – ¾ cup warm water

FRIJOLES:

1 cup dried black kidney beans, or a
   2½ cup can pinto or red kidney beans

1 bay leaf

1 tablespoon virgin olive oil

1 red onion, chopped

3 garlic cloves, crushed

1 red chili, finely chopped (seeded for
   a milder dish)

fine sea salt and freshly ground black pepper

sprigs of basil, for garnish

VEGETABLE FILLING:

2 large onions, sliced

1-2 red chiles, finely chopped

3 garlic cloves, crushed

juice of 2 limes

2 tablespoons chopped fresh cilantro

4 large red bell peppers, cored, seeded, and cut
   into strips

4 large yellow bell peppers, cored, seeded, and cut
   into strips

4 large zucchini cut into thin strips

2 tablespoons extra-virgin olive oil

fine sea salt and freshly ground black pepper

2 tablespoons chopped fresh cilantro or
   basil, for garnish

DIPS:

2 ripe avocados

juice of 1 lime

1 cup sour cream

1 bunch of chives, finely snipped

This translates as "Little packages and refried beans" accompanied by avocado and lime dip, sour cream, and chives and salsa.

It is a wonderful family dish so long as you don't go too mad on the chiles. Any food that involves participation at the meal table apart from normal eating with a knife and fork always seems to be automatically successful. Children and parents alike will enjoy assembling their own food in this vegetarian version of a Mexican favorite.

Ensure that everyone is seated, relaxed, and ready for the dish to arrive, while you cook the vegetables, as they are best eaten hot and tend to cool quite quickly. If possible, keep them warm in a dish over a candle or a spirit burner.

Frijoles is a traditional Mexican dish sometimes called Refritos (Refried Beans). It is actually best made in advance and re-heated, giving the flavors a chance to develop. It will keep well for up to 4 days, covered, in a refrigerator. Frijoles are commonly made with black kidney beans but red kidney beans and pinto beans are equally tasty, although not quite so eye-catching.

1 To make the tortillas, put the flour and salt in a bowl, and rub in the fat to form a crumb-textured mixture. Slowly add the warm water, mixing in to form a soft dough.

2 Place the dough on a lightly floured surface and knead for 1 minute. Divide into 12 pieces and cover with a damp cloth to prevent it from drying out. Roll out each piece into a 6-inch diameter circle. Dust off any excess flour and stack on a plate, placing a piece of paper towel between each tortilla to prevent them from sticking together.

3 Heat a heavy-bottom skillet until very hot—cure it with salt if necessary to prevent sticking. (See note below.) Cook the tortillas for 1 minute on each side or until patchy-brown. It may be necessary to wipe the pan between tortillas to avoid any excess flour burning. Once cooked, place them in an ovenproof dish covered with a damp cloth to keep them moist.

4 If using dried beans for the frijoles, put them in a deep saucepan and cover with double their volume of water, bring to a boil quickly, then boil rapidly for 10 minutes. Set the beans aside and let them soak overnight or for at least 12 hours.

5 Put the beans into fresh water with the bay leaf, bring to a boil, cover and simmer for 1-1½ hours, or until very tender but not mushy. While they are cooking, heat the oil in a pan. Add the onion, garlic, and chili, and cook until the onion has softened—be careful not to burn them.

6 Drain the cooked beans, reserving the cooking liquid, and add to the onion mixture, or add the canned beans, if using, instead. Mash with a potato masher, adding a little of the bean cooking liquid to make a moist consistency. (Don't use a food processor here as the resulting purée would be disappointing.) Season and set aside to cool.

7 For the vegetable filling, combine all the ingredients in a bowl, cover, and let marinade in the refrigerator overnight. Ten minutes before serving, remove the vegetables from the marinade and place in a hot skillet and stir-fry for 5-6 minutes, or until the onions are starting to soften. If it's a bit dry add a little of the marinade.

8 For the two dips, simply scoop out the flesh of the avocados, add the lime juice, season, and place in a serving dish. Combine the sour cream and chives and serve in another dish.

9 To serve the meal, re-heat the beans in a low oven, a microwave or, even better, refry them and serve in a dish garnished with basil sprigs. The tortillas may be reheated in a hot oven or in a steaming basket. Place the dips, beans, and tortillas on the table and serve the vegetables.

10 To assemble, place a hot tortilla on your plate, add some vegetables, a good dollop of frijoles, and top with any combination of the accompaniments. Simply roll it up and enjoy it! The meal could be stretched with the addition of salads, nachos, cheese, or even a rice dish, all washed down with Mexican beer for the adults and perhaps fresh lime and lemonade for the children.

Note:

To cure a skillet with salt, heat the pan until hot. Add salt to cover the bottom of the pan, and using paper towels, rub into the pan until clean. Wipe the pan and use.

Overleaf Left- MEXICAN FAJITAS AND FRIJOLES *Right-*TIJUANA FRUIT SALSA

Tomato and Cilantro Salsa

1 small red onion, finely chopped

2 tablespoons chopped fresh cilantro

2 garlic cloves, crushed

1 cup fresh, ripe tomatoes, peeled,
    seeded, and chopped

a dash of white wine vinegar and/or brown sugar,
    to taste

fine sea salt and freshly ground black pepper

cilantro leaves, for garnish

1 Combine the onion, cilantro, garlic, and a small amount of the tomatoes in a blender or food processor and blend for about 10 seconds. Then fold the mixture into the rest of the tomatoes, season, and adjust the acidity. If it is too sweet, add a little white wine vinegar; if too sharp, add a little brown sugar.

2 Pour the salsa into a serving dish, season, and garnish with cilantro leaves. Serve as an accompaniment to Fajitas and Frijoles (see page 134).

Tijuana Fruit Salsa

1 small ripe pineapple, cut into ½-inch cubes

1 ripe mango, skinned, pitted, and cubed

1 ripe banana, sliced

4 passion fruits, pulp of

1 small ripe Galia or other orange-fleshed melon,
    cut into chunks

3 tablespoons fresh lime juice

⅓ cup fresh orange juice

4 mint leaves

After a filling and spicy main course, taste buds cry out to be cleansed and cooled. This dessert has a truly tropical feel and is excellent served with vanilla ice cream or smooth and creamy plain yogurt.

1 Combine the fruit and fruit juices in a glass serving bowl well in advance to allow the flavors to mingle. Serve well chilled and garnished with fresh mint.

FEAST TWO

Latkes are the most simple of all crêpes made most commonly from mashed potato. They are generally accredited to northern Europe–Poland, Germany, and Russia in particular–but are made in one form or another throughout the world. (There are wonderful street vendors in Morocco who sell tiny potato crêpes flavored with garlic, fried in olive oil, and served with a searing hot chili sauce.) Like all good food forms they will adjust to seasons, climates, and may be added to and accompanied by a myriad of different things, and what is most important in the context of this book, is that children love them!

These spinach latkes, accompanied by a delicious wild mushroom and cheese sauce, and followed by a sumptuous dessert, is the perfect meal for any type of gathering; be it family or friends.

Serves 4

Spinach Latkes with Wild Mushroom and Three-Cheese Sauce

Sticky Apple and Lemon Pudding

Spinach Latkes with Wild Mushroom and Three-Cheese Sauce

LATKES:

¼ cup extra-virgin olive oil

4 shallots, finely sliced

2 teaspoons mustard seeds

2 carrots, shredded

1 cup fresh spinach, stalks removed and chopped

4 cups mashed potato

1 teaspoon lemon juice

fine sea salt and freshly ground black pepper

SAUCE:

2 tablespoons (¼ stick) butter

4 cups mushrooms (such as oyster mushrooms, chanterelle or plain flat mushrooms)

2 cups heavy cream

2 cups Fontina cheese, cut into small pieces

¾ cup Gorgonzola cheese, cut into small pieces

2 garlic cloves, finely chopped

1 tablespoon chopped fresh basil

½ cup Parmesan cheese, shredded

Latkes can be made a day in advance and stored uncooked in the refrigerator separated by small squares of wax paper.

1 To make the latkes, heat 2 tablespoons of the olive oil in a large saucepan. Cook the shallots until beginning to soften. Add the mustard seeds and let pop; stir in the carrots and spinach, and cook until soft. Try to evaporate as much of the water from the spinach as possible, stirring continuously to avoid burning.

2 When the carrots are cooked but still have some "bite," remove from the heat and fold in the mashed potato, lemon juice, and seasoning to form an even consistency. Let the mixture cool.

3 Using floured hands, shape the mixture into 8 round patties.

4 Heat enough of the remaining oil in a saucepan and cook the latkes for 5 minutes on each side until golden brown.

5 For the sauce, heat the butter in a heavy-bottom skillet, add the mushrooms, season and cook for about 5 minutes. Remove the mushrooms from the pan with a slotted spoon and set aside. Over a high heat reduce the liquid left in the pan to a spoonful.

6 In a separate saucepan bring the cream to gently boiling and let it reduce by half. Reduce the heat to very low and add the Fontina, Gorgonzola, garlic, and basil. Finally, stir in the mushrooms. Reduce the liquid a little more. Adjust the seasoning and just before serving add the Parmesan.

7 Serve the latkes with a wedge of lemon and a nice crisp salad and/or some plainly cooked vegetables and, of course, the sauce.

Sticky Apple and Lemon Pudding

½ cup (1 stick) unsalted butter

2 pounds cooking apples, peeled, cored,
    and chopped

⅓ cup raisins

2 heaped tablespoons light brown sugar

dash of rum (optional)

½ cup soft brown sugar

3 eggs (large) from free-range chickens, separated,
    the yolks beaten

1 teaspoon ground cinnamon

shredded rind and juice of 2 lemons

3 tablespoons unbleached self-rising white flour

pinch of salt

½ teaspoon cream of tartar

½ cup milk

whipped cream, to serve

This is a delicious pudding, although the addition of fresh whipped cream will make it a feast.

1 Melt ¼ cup (½ stick) of the butter in a heavy-bottom saucepan, add the apples, raisins, light brown sugar, and a dash of rum, if using. Stir fry for 2 minutes, then transfer the mixture to an 8-inch soufflé dish. Let cool.

2 Beat the remaining butter and soft brown sugar together in a bowl until light and fluffy. Gradually add the egg yolks. When the mixture is well combined stir in the ground cinnamon, lemon juice, and rind. Sift in the flour with the salt, cream of tartar, and then slowly add the milk. Mix until the mixture is smooth.

3 Beat the egg whites in a clean, grease-free bowl until soft peaks form, then fold into the rest of the mixture. Pour over the apples and place straight in a preheated oven, 350°F. Cook until well risen and firm to the touch, about 40-50 minutes. Serve with whipped cream.

FEAST THREE

Cooking with the season is no longer the prerequisite it was even 50 years ago. But when cooking this meal try to use fruit and vegetables that are in season. August/September would be ideal in England, when bell peppers are plump and sweet, and peaches (almost) ripe and juicy, and still warm from their trees in southern Europe. It's a perfect meal after a long, hot, summer day. Whatever you do, don't tell the children it's goat's cheese until they have finished eating it!

Serves 4

Warm Italian Roast Salad with Goat's Cheese and Croutons

Italian Peach Tart
Muscat Zabaglioni

Warm Italian Roast Salad with Goat's Cheese and Croutons

1 large yellow bell pepper, cored, seeded, and cut into
  thick strips
1 large green bell pepper, cored, seeded, and cut into
  thick strips
6 shallots, peeled and trimmed
a little dried thyme or oregano, for sprinkling
3 garlic cloves, crushed
½ cup extra-virgin olive oil, plus extra
  for brushing
3 tablespoons white wine vinegar
1 dessertspoon soft brown sugar
6 tomatoes, peeled, seeded, and cut into strips
3 tablespoons chopped fresh basil
3 cups organic white spirelli pasta
1½ cups goat's cheese, crumbled
3 cups garlic croutons
12 olives, halved and pitted
fine sea salt and freshly ground black pepper

Here's a salad that's a meal in itself. "Roast salad," I hear you say, "sounds a bit improbable." Read on and all will be revealed.
1 Brush the peppers and shallots with a little olive oil. Season with salt and pepper and some thyme or oregano, if you like. Place in a roasting pan in a preheated oven, 425°F, for 30-40 minutes or until tender.
2 Meanwhile, mix together the garlic, the ½ cup of oil, the vinegar, sugar, and seasoning in a bowl. Stir in the tomatoes, then gently stir in the basil.
3 Cook the spirelli in a large saucepan of boiling water until *al dente*. Drain and combine immediately with the tomato and basil dressing. Add the warm peppers and shallots, then top with the goat's cheese, warm garlic croutons, and the olives.
4 Serve with chunks of fresh Italian bread or broiled polenta.

Overleaf Left—WARM ITALIAN ROAST SALAD WITH GOAT'S CHEESE AND CROUTONS *Right*—ITALIAN PEACH TART

Italian Peach Tart

⅝ cup (1½ sticks) unsalted butter

¼ pound filo pastry

1⅓ cups mascarpone cheese

½ cup cream cheese

½ teaspoon vanilla extract

3 tablespoons clear honey

rind and juice of 1 small lime

2 pounds peaches, peeled if you like, pitted, and
thickly sliced

3 tablespoons Moscato white wine

½ cup chocolate shavings, for decoration

*A light main dish demands a substantial dessert like this
one. Try this tart using any orchard fruit. Choose peaches
that are firm, yielding very slightly, unblemished, and not
over-ripe.*

1 Gently melt ¼ cup (½ stick) of the butter and brush some
on to the bottom of a 9-inch loose-based fluted pie pan; lay
a sheet of filo pastry over it. Brush the pastry sheet with
more melted butter and then lay another sheet of pastry on
top. Repeat this process until all the filo has been used.

2 Line the pastry shell with wax paper and fill with ceramic baking beans. Bake blind in a preheated oven, 400°F, for
10 minutes before removing the beans and wax paper.
Brush the pastry shell with more butter and finish cooking,
about another 5-6 minutes. Set aside to cool.

3 Meanwhile, mix together the mascarpone, cream cheese,
vanilla extract, honey, lime juice, and rind in a small bowl.

4 Melt the remaining butter in a large skillet. Sauté the
peaches for about 3 minutes, then add the wine and reduce
it to a thick syrup. Cook the peaches over a high heat until
caramelized and almost dry.

5 Spread the cream cheese mixture over the filo pastry base
and top with the peaches. Decorate with chocolate shavings and serve warm or chilled with whipped cream.

Muscat Zabaglioni

3 egg yolks from free-range chickens

3 tablespoons soft brown sugar

¼ cup Muscat wine

½ cup heavy cream

*The perfumed sweetness of Muscat is the perfect accompa-
niment to peaches or other fruity desserts. Muscat
Zabaglioni can be also be served as a dessert in its own
right. It is no more difficult to make than custard.*

1 In a heatproof bowl beat the egg yolks with the sugar until
pale and fluffy.

2 Put the bowl above a saucepan of boiling water and gradually add the wine, whisking frequently. When the sauce
has thickened without curdling set it aside to cool.

3 Beat the cream until it forms soft peaks, then beat in the
Muscat sauce. Chill well before serving.

FEAST FOUR

This recipe is guaranteed to capture your children's attention. Your main problem will be getting them to slow down and eat at a pace which allows the rest of the family to have some. There should be penalties for dropping bits of bread or vegetables in the fondue (especially washing up or stacking the dishwasher)–likewise for dripping fondue onto the tablecloth.

Serves 4

Herby Fondue
Celeriac and Carrot Salad

Chocolate Coffee Cake

Herby Fondue

2 tablespoons (¼ stick) butter

1 small onion, chopped

¼ cup unbleached all-purpose white flour

1 cup whole milk

1 tablespoon chopped fresh basil

1 tablespoon chopped fresh parsley

1 tablespoon chopped fresh chervil

1 tablespoon snipped fresh chives

½ cup dry white wine

2 cups Gruyère cheese, shredded

2 cups Emmenthal or Edam cheese, shredded

1 tablespoon brandy or kirsch

finely ground nutmeg

pinch of cayenne pepper

1 garlic clove, peeled and halved

fine sea salt and freshly ground black pepper

TO SERVE:

large loaf of crusty bread, cut into 1-inch cubes

2¼ cups cooked vegetables (such as cauliflower or broccoli flowerets, carrot sticks, celery, bell peppers, or new potatoes)

This is probably really only suitable for children over 8 although, of course, you can set aside little bits of cool fondue for your younger ones. It will help to have fondue equipment for this dish–earthenware sets are best.

1 Melt the butter in a deep, heavy-bottom saucepan. Add the chopped onion and cook until beginning to soften. Stir in the flour and cook for about 1 minute. Gradually stir in the milk to make a white sauce. Season to taste.

2 Stir the herbs into the sauce then gradually add the white wine, being careful not to curdle the sauce. Add the remaining ingredients except the garlic. Rub the inside of your fondue dish with the cut garlic and pour in the fondue. Keep warm over a candle or spirit burner.

3 Serve, using fondue forks to dip the bread and vegetables into the fondue.

Celeriac and Carrot Salad

8 ounces carrot, coarsely shredded

1 small celeriac, peeled and cut into julienne strips

½ cup large, sweet raisins

½ cup toasted pumpkin seeds

DRESSING:

4 tablespoons freshly squeezed lemon juice

½ cup sunflower oil

3 teaspoons clear honey

fine sea salt and freshly ground black pepper

1 tablespoon Dijon mustard

⅓ cup mayonnaise

Celeriac is a lovely vegetable–it just looks ugly! It's best raw and young but still tastes good old and cooked. As well as in salads, soups, and stews, it's also great as a side dish in its own right.

1 Make the dressing by combining the lemon juice, oil, honey and seasoning in a jar with a tight-fitting lid.

2 Fold the Dijon mustard into the mayonnaise.

3 Quickly toss the shredded carrot and celeriac strips in the lemon and honey dressing. It should be moist, not wet.

4 Fold the raisins and toasted pumpkin seeds into the mixture and finally add the mustard mayonnaise. Refrigerate the salad at least 30 minutes before serving.

Chocolate Coffee Cake

½ pound unsweetened chocolate, broken into pieces

1 tablespoon instant coffee granules

1 cup light brown sugar

5 eggs from free-range chickens, separated

2 cups ground almonds

TOPPING:

1 cup heavy cream, whipped

1 tablespoon dark rum

sifted cocoa powder, for sprinkling

After a rich main course, sometimes the only flavor that can fight back is chocolate. Chocolate and coffee make an excellent partnership.

1 Melt the chocolate in a heatproof bowl over a large heavy-bottom saucepan of gently boiling water, whisk in the instant coffee granules and remove from the heat.

2 Cream the sugar and egg yolks together in a bowl until light and fluffy. Stir in the almonds, melted chocolate, and coffee. Beat well together.

3 Beat the egg whites in a clean grease-free bowl until stiff, then fold into the chocolate and coffee mixture. Pour into a greased 9-inch cake pan and bake in a preheated oven, 350°F, for 55 minutes until firm to the touch. Leave for a few minutes before turning out onto a wire rack.

4 When cool, top with the whipped cream into which a little rum has been beaten, and sprinkle the cake with the sifted cocoa powder.

Makes a 9-inch cake

FEAST FIVE

This feast would make a lovely Sunday lunch or brunch as it is healthy and the children will love it. Broiled asparagus might be a new experience for British children but it's an old art form in the USA. Boston Beans are my favorite way of cooking beans and probably were the first vegetarian dish I ever cooked.

Serves 4

Ranch-Style Rösti
Boston Baked Beans
Broiled Asparagus

Muffled Plums
Treacle Sauce

Ranch-Style Rösti

1 pound Maris Piper potatoes
8 ounces celeriac
1 cup vegetarian Cheddar cheese, shredded
3 tablespoons extra-virgin olive oil
2 teaspoons chopped fresh thyme
2 tablespoons chopped fresh parsley
½ teaspoon cayenne pepper
4 eggs (large) from free-range chickens
fine sea salt and freshly ground black pepper

1 Par-cook the potatoes and celeriac in a large pan of salted boiling water for 10 minutes. Drain, cool and peel, then grate into a bowl. Stir the cheese into the potatoes, then add the oil, herbs and seasoning.
2 Spoon the mixture into a lightly oiled baking dish or 4 individual ovenproof dishes—do not compress the mixture. Make 4 slight hollows in the potato, if using one large dish. Bake in a preheated oven, 400°F, for 20 minutes then remove and break an egg into each dish or the hollows in the one dish. Return to the oven for a further 10 minutes or until the eggs have just set. Serve immediately.

Boston Baked Beans

2½ cups dried borlotti beans
1 large onion, chopped
2 celery stalks, chopped
4 garlic cloves, crushed
1 green chili, chopped
1 bay leaf
2 cinnamon sticks
3 tablespoons molasses
1 tablespoon soft brown sugar
¼ cup tomato paste
¼ cup whole grain mustard
¼ cup malt vinegar
fine sea salt and freshly ground black pepper
3 tablespoons chopped fresh parsley, for garnish

Best cooked and prepared a day ahead, these make excellent accompaniments to all kinds of main dishes and are good on their own, with bread and salsa. They take quite a lot of cooking

Overleaf Left—BROILED ASPARAGUS, BOSTON BAKED BEANS
Right—RANCH-STYLE RÖSTI

so make plenty and freeze what you don't use. If borlotti beans are unavailable, haricot and kidney beans are perfectly good substitutes.

1 Bring the beans to a boil in a large saucepan of water. Cook rapidly for 10 minutes, skim them if necessary, then simmer for 45 minutes or until tender.

2 Drain the beans and place in a casserole dish. Add the rest of the ingredients to the beans, cover, and bake in a preheated oven, 300°F, for about 4 hours or until soft, thick, and saucy. Serve the beans hot or cold.

Broiled Asparagus

20 asparagus stalks (grade 1)
¼ cup extra-virgin olive oil
3 tablespoons lemon juice
fine sea salt and freshly ground black pepper

Once again the children surprisingly love asparagus. If you prefer, steam the asparagus and serve with a simple lemon butter sauce.

1 Brush the asparagus with some of the olive oil, making sure that each stalk is well coated, and season to taste. Broil slowly under a low heat for about 5 minutes or until the tip of a knife inserted tells you they are done.

2 Serve the asparagus with more fruity olive oil and a splash of lemon juice.

Muffled Plums

¾ cup (1½ sticks) butter, softened
¾ cup light brown sugar
1 teaspoon ground ginger
1 pound cooking plums or greengages, halved and pitted
2 eggs (large) from free-range chickens, beaten
1 cup unbleached white self-rising flour
1 teaspoon baking powder
½ cup regular oats
1 teaspoon ground cinnamon
¼ cup milk

In this case "muffle" has many applications, but most of all it's the noise you make when you're eating them! Any fruit or combination of fruit, especially orchard fruit, could be used in place of the plums.

1 Melt ¼ cup (½ stick) of the butter with ¼ cup of the sugar and the ginger together in a small saucepan.

2 Place the plums in a 4-cup shallow ovenproof dish and pour the melted butter, sugar, and ground ginger over.

3 Beat the remaining butter and sugar together in a bowl until light and fluffy, gradually add the eggs, then fold in the flour, baking powder, oats, and cinnamon. Finally, beat in the milk. Spread the mixture over the plums. Bake for about 30 minutes in a preheated oven, 375°F, until firm.

4 Serve hot with fresh vanilla custard, cream, ice cream, or Treacle Sauce (see below).

Treacle Sauce

3 tablespoons (⅓ stick) butter
½ cup light brown sugar
1 tablespoon molasses
⅓ cup heavy cream

1 Heat the butter, sugar, and molasses together in a small saucepan until melted, then stir in the cream. Bring the mixture to the boil gently and let reduce until it reaches a thick, creamy consistency.

FEAST SIX

Have your very own vegetarian Balti dinner or lunch at home. The essence of a "Balti" meal is two contrasting curries served not with rice but with naan bread to scoop up mouthfuls of the delicious curry. Once again this will be a guaranteed success with the whole family, and if the older members prefer a bit more spice than the younger ones, then it's easy just to make another more spicy dish specifically for them.

Traditionally, Balti food comes from Baltistan, a remote part of Pakistan. The food was cooked in woks, which it is believed were inherited into the culture of the wandering Baltis from the Chinese. It's nice to use the traditional individual iron Balti dishes for your meal but they will act more as serving receptacles than as a means of cooking.

Serves 4

Red Onion and Mint Raita
Naan Bread
Balti Sauce
Medium Eggplant and Potato Balti
Mushroom and Zucchini Korma

Mango Kulfi

Red Onion and Mint Raita

2 red onions, finely chopped

pinch of chili powder

squeeze of lemon juice

⅓ cup chopped fresh mint

1 tablespoon chopped fresh cilantro

1 teaspoon mustard powder

1 teaspoon ground cumin

½ teaspoon finely shredded fresh ginger root

1 cup plain yogurt, stirred

¼ cup sour cream

fine sea salt and finely ground black pepper

8 poppadums, to serve

Just something for dipping poppadums into, to nibble on while waiting for the main dish to arrive.

1 Mix all the ingredients together well and chill before serving, accompanied by the poppadums for dipping into the raita.

Naan Bread

1 tablespoon light brown sugar

¾ cake compressed yeast

1 cup tepid milk

⅓ cup (¾ stick) butter

4 cups unbleached white bread flour

1 teaspoon sea salt

1 tablespoon chopped fresh cilantro

Overleaf Left—RED ONION AND MINT RAITA, NAAN BREAD *Right*—MANGO KULFI, MEDIUM EGGPLANT AND POTATO BALTI, MUSHROOM AND ZUCCHINI KORMA.

Normally cooked in a tandoori oven, a similar result can be achieved at home with a hot broiler.

1 Mix the sugar and yeast in a small jug with ⅓ cup of the warm milk. Cover and set aside in a warm place for 10 minutes until frothing.

2 Meanwhile, rub ¼ cup (½ stick) of the butter into the flour and salt in a bowl and melt the remaining butter, setting it aside. When the yeast is frothy add it to the flour mixture and gradually add the rest of the milk. Mix well to form a dough. Put it on to a lightly floured work surface and knead for 10 minutes. Place in an oiled bowl, cover the bowl with plastic wrap, and place in a warm, dry, draft-free place for 1 hour or until doubled in bulk.

3 Knock back the dough and divide into 4. Roll each piece out into a large, rough, thin circle. Prick all over with a fork and press the cilantro into the surface.

4 Heat a baking sheet under a hot broiler. When hot, place a naan on it and broil for a few minutes each side until just starting to brown. Brush with the melted butter, wrap in foil, and keep warm in a low oven while cooking the rest. Naan bread are best served warm.

Balti Sauce

3 red onions, finely chopped

3 garlic cloves, crushed

2 green chiles, seeded and chopped

1-inch piece of fresh ginger root, shredded

⅓ cup ghee, or clarified butter

1 teaspoon mustard powder

1 teaspoon ground fenugreek

½ teaspoon ground cumin

1 tablespoon ground turmeric

½ tablespoon paprika

1 tablespoon ground coriander

1 teaspoon ground cinnamon

5 whole cardamoms, crushed

5 whole cloves

shredded rind and juice of 1 lemon

¼ cup tomato paste

2 cups water or vegetable stock

fine sea salt and freshly ground black pepper

This is the key to Balti entertaining–a sauce which can be added to almost anything.

1 In a large heavy-bottom saucepan, cook the onions, garlic, chiles, and ginger in the ghee or butter for 8 minutes. Add the spices and stir fry for 1 minute. Add the remaining ingredients, bring to a boil, and simmer for 45 minutes.

2 Pass the sauce through a fine strainer and adjust the seasoning to taste. Let cool, then store in the refrigerator until ready to use. It will keep for several days.

Makes 2 cups

Medium Eggplant and Potato Balti

1 onion, sliced

1 tablespoon fennel seeds

1 tablespoon black mustard seeds

¼ cup ghee or vegetable oil

1 pound eggplant, cut into chunks

2 red bell peppers, cored, seeded, and cut into
   1-inch squares

1½ cups green beans, topped, tailed, halved, and
   blanched

3 cups new potatoes, cooked and halved

1½ cups okra, blanched

1 quantity Balti Sauce (see opposite)

1½ cups tomatoes, peeled, seeded,
   and chopped

½ cup fresh sweet basil, chopped

fine sea salt and freshly ground black pepper

1 In a large saucepan, cook the onion and seeds together in the ghee or oil until the seeds pop. Add the eggplant and cook for 5 minutes. Add the peppers, beans, potatoes, and okra, and cook for a further 10 minutes.

2 Stir in the Balti sauce and bring to a boil. Fold in the chopped tomatoes and basil, adjust the seasoning to taste, and cook for a further 4 minutes, before ready to serve.

Mushroom and Zucchini Korma

1 onion, chopped
3 tablespoons ghee, or clarified butter
6 cups button mushrooms
¾ quantity Balti Sauce (see page 154)
⅓ cup coconut cream
½ cup ground almonds
1 pound zucchini, topped, tailed, and sliced
½ cup heavy cream
⅓ cup chopped fresh cilantro
fine sea salt and freshly ground black pepper
½ cup almond flakes, toasted, for garnish

This is a startling contrast to the previous dish! Use the tiniest mushrooms you can find.

1 In a saucepan, cook the chopped onion in the ghee over a high heat for 1-2 minutes, add the mushrooms, and cook for a further 3 minutes.

2 Stir in the Balti sauce, coconut cream, and ground almonds, and bring to a boil. Add the sliced zucchini and cook gently for a further 8 minutes. Stir in the cream and cook for a further 2 minutes. Add the cilantro and seasoning, and serve garnished with the almond flakes.

Mango Kulfi

1¼ cups light cream
¼ cup light brown sugar
5 green cardamoms, crushed
shredded rind of 1 lemon
1 large ripe mango, about 1½ cups, peeled and pitted
½ cup pistachio nuts, chopped, for garnish

I think that this is one of the nicest ice creams in the world! Vegans could use soya milk and extra sweetener in place of the single cream.

1 Warm the cream in a small saucepan together with the sugar, cardamoms, and lemon rind. As soon as the sugar dissolves, remove the pan from the heat. Allow the mixture to cool and infuse, then strain.

2 In a blender or food processor, blend the mango and cream together to a smooth texture. Pour into a shallow freezerproof plastic container and freeze for about 1½ hours. Stir the mixture after this time—it should be beginning to freeze. If desired, pour the kulfi into cleaned yogurt pots. Return to the freezer until frozen solid.

3 Serve the kulfi garnished with the chopped pistachios.

INDEX

Page numbers in italic refer to illustrations

Bake blind – A method of baking to ensure a crisp dough crust. Line a prepared dough pan with crumpled foil or wax paper, fill with baking beans, peas or dried pasta and bake in a preheated oven for 10-15 minutes. Remove the beans and foil and return the dough to the oven for 5 minutes or until brown.

Barley Miso – A type of barley stock.

Bok choy – Also known as bài-cái; Chinese vegetable in the mustard family with dark green leaves and white stalks.

Borlotti Beans – An Italian bean; oval with a pink-brownish skin. Can substitute any other bean avaliable such as white kidney beans or navy beans.

Cardamom – Related to ginger, an Indian spice used to flavor rice, meat, noodles and cakes.

Celeriac – Also known as turnip-root celery; used raw or cooked, a large turnip-shaped root.

Ceps – Also known as cépes or funghi porcini; a variety of wild mushrooms with tubes under cap instead of gills.

Clear honey – Also known as pure honey.

Dolcelatte – A sweet Italian cheese.

Fenugreek – Used fresh or dried, this Mediterranean plant belongs to the pea family and is used in curries, chutneys, pickles, and meat dishes.

Garam Masala – An Indian spice of coriander, cloves, cinnamon, cumin, and black pepper.

Ghee – A clarified fat used in Indian cooking.

Grana Padano – A very hard Italian cow's cheese, very similar to Pamesan.

Mango chutney – A sweet and sour relish made of mango, cooked in vinegar, salt and spices until it achieves a jam-like consistency. Chutneys can be made from a variety of vegetables and fruits and are served with meat and curry dishes.

Mascarpone – A soft Italian cheese used in many desserts.

Mirin – A Japanese sweet white wine.

Pakora batter – Indian fritter batter made of chick-pea flour, onion, and other ingredients including chicken and spices.

Poppadums – Indian; Also known as pappadam; large thin wafers made from lentil flour and fried in oil. Eaten whole or crushed and sprinkled over food.

Quark – Also known as curds; a slightly sour low-fat cottage cheese.

Rocket – Also known as arugula.

Shoyu – Soy sauce.

Swede – Also known as Swedish turnip; a large firm turnip, yellowish-orange in color.

Tahini – Middle Eastern sesame seed paste.

Tempeh – Also known as tempe; fermented soy-bean cake.

Tofu – Soybean curd; neutral in taste and high in protein, it is used in many Far Eastern dishes.

Tomato passata – Sieved tomatoes, it is thicker than tomato paste.

Vegan – An adherent of veganism, a strict form of vegetarianism based upon eating only plants and plant products.

Vegan margarine – Margarine made without dairy products.

Vegetarian mature Cheddar – An aged Cheddar cheese made without animal fats or oils.

Vegetarian Parmesan – Parmesan made without animal fats or oils.

Vegetarian Worcestershire – A Worcestershire sauce made without animal based fat or oil.